KNOWLEDGE POWERS WISDOM EMPOWERS

JOYRAM

INDIA • SINGAPORE • MALAYSIA

ISBN 979-8-89067-804-1

Contents

Foreword

This book is akin to my first ever book "Take Whatever You Want" which I published in 2020 under the penname 'Ram'. However, the orientation of this book is slightly different from my earlier book. While my first book covered my thoughts from certain angles, this book contains my thoughts from different perspectives. In addition to the thoughts, I have brought out a variety of humour. The unique combination of thoughts and humour is the speciality of this book.

The book is so designed that my thoughts and humour are shared alternatively. This, I hope, would make the readers get engrossed in my thoughts and in the next moment, smile and burst into laughter when reading the humour episode that follows the thought. In spite of applying the knowledge we gain in every walk of our life, we continue to get stuck up and stranded at busy psychological junctions like problems, worries, disappointments, failures etc. As a self-made doctor of humour, I strongly advocate that one should laugh away their problems and worries. I earnestly believe that is how we empower our wisdom to act, bloom and blossom in every life situation.

In a way, what I offer in this food court is a blend of green and fruit salad. My thoughts are like a health-friendly green salad mix of cucumber, tomato, onion, carrot etc. with a pinch of sour but sure taste. My humour episodes are like a dessert of fruit salad mix of sweet mangos, apples, bananas, pineapple, pomegranates, grapes etc. with occasional strange but pure taste.

Every thought in this book is borne out of either my experience or conviction. I am sure readers will have something to gain from my thoughts from the point of life learning. In the same way, readers will find my humour, triggers a pleasant smile, if not roaring laughter. If this twin objective is achieved, even in minuscule, I would consider the purpose of this book as accomplished.

– Joyram

Thought
Friendship

Life begins with a mother and ends with a spouse. In between these two relationships, one comes across a plethora of relationships and associations. Relatives, friends, colleagues, and neighbours to mention a few.

The relationship of blood is, no doubt, bondage for life. Children, siblings, and kith and kin fit in this vital category. The relationships with neighbours and colleagues, in general, are due to necessity rather than interest. As long as one works in an organization, the association with colleagues continues. Till such time we remain as neighbours to our neighbours and vice versa the association of neighbours prolongs.

In addition to the above, there is one important association called 'Friendship'. Friends for the heck of it are plenty. It may be in the hundreds. Friends for the sake of friends are just ordinary but not true friends because of the tag of expectations. What stands distinct is true friendship, an association of soulful bondage. As opposed to ordinary friendships, true friendships are built over a period of time with trust, confidence, and reliability as key foundations.

In anyone's life, such real friendships can be counted on fingers. The thumb rule is one may have one or two best friends in a lifetime. We also come across soulful friend groups of four to even six as well which is a rare phenomenon, of course. The most spectacular aspect of true friendship is the absence of status and ego. There are best friends in proximity to each other, like childhood friendships. But once built strongly, friendship knows no bounds. Geographical distances, matrimonial status, social and professional status, nothing like these matters.

A true friendship is one where the two persons involved treat each other as part of their own soul. If one has even one such friend in life, that person is really blessed. No other bondage or relationship can deliver that kind of real satisfaction, found between two thick friends. Nobody and no other relationship on earth can substitute the heartfelt togetherness spent while being with a true friend.

I hope you are one such blessed person.

Thought
There is nothing like nothing

In anything and everything there's something. If you get bruised by falling on the sharp-edged stones and if someone enquires "What happened to your hand and face? "You say "It is nothing, just two small bruises ". It is clear that there is some bruise but we prefer not to make the bruises as significant. This analogy holds good for everything.

If one's purse is lifted, one would say "It is nothing, just a two thousand rupees and two credit cards. For everything that is insignificant to us, we either don't mind such things or at least pretend so. If we could simulate this 'nothing' at the macro level, for everything that costs the economy and lives we tend to say "It is nothing compared to what happened twenty years ago."

So, there is something in everything. The only question is how big or small, how important or insignificant one's something is. One school of philosophy and another scientific analysis concludes that everything in this universe has popped out from the so called nothingness. What could be this nothingness?

The void which we could see in the vast space in the sky appears to be nothing. But is it not void of something? Does zero mean nothing? That is why I am compelled to opine that there is something, extraordinarily powerful, invisible, and invincible energy, pervading this entire universe, which we perceive as something like God or Nature or Nothing.

Thought
Even if takes the extra mile, smile

Smile for yourself as much so that you can give more and more genuine smile packs to others!

To say this is so easy but doing it calls for dedicated efforts because to smile innocently is A beautiful act of service!

To deliver an unadulterated smile, your mind should be as refined and pure as crystal-clear water

To bring your mind to such a level, you need to forget the past, every bitter memory that shakes Your balance!

To do that calls for the Good Samaritan acts of giving to the needy, forgiving people, accepting them as they are, and eradicating the core of hatred feelings!

To start the above process, you need to revitalize your mind battery and recharge it with more and more guts and wits of positive energy!

Doing these with a commitment and observing your every single act of thought and deed, will and must bring fruitful rewards to you and that will be an achievement in your life, indeed!

In the process, you would be smiling beautifully, at yourself and at others, like the charming colourful dangling blooming flowers!

Thought
Being certain about happiness

Having enjoyed the inevitable sufferings, having suffered the indispensable enjoyments, having experienced the unpredictable nature of life, having been born on numerous occasions whenever elevated by positive spirits, having died helplessly many times, whenever struck by apprehensions of evaporating fears, worries, tragedies, having discovered on innumerable occasions that life is short-tenure gambling, having been convinced that the meaning of life is an undeniable mystery, why continue to think and behave like any other ordinary human being, dwindling in uncertainty, instead of being certain about the happiness that is present in every present moment in you that is invariably certain.

Thought
Observe your breathing

Observe yourself closely by watching your breathing. Be aware of the depth of your thoughts. While observing the thoughts, avoid getting entangled with them. It will be quite difficult to keep away from thoughts. But by trying to observe your breathing, you will be gradually able to reduce the number of thoughts and their intensity. In this direction, lay guts and courage as the strong basement. Most of the time, it is either the past or future that sweeps your thoughts. You'll agree with this when you observe your thoughts with all awareness. Once you know the mantra for joy is to stay in the present, then make use of this mental exercise to live consciously in the present state.

Humour
Rapid-fire quiz

Question: Who is a father?
Answer: The one who is the son of his father
Question: Define air
Answer: All India Radio or Anything In Random
Question: Who is a cashier?
Answer: The one with plenty of cash who cannot spend it on himself
Question: Why do we eat?
Answer: To enable one to cook again
Question: Why do we marry the opposite gender?
Answer: In order to create more and more blunders
Question: Why do we go to school?
Answer: To become a literate fool
Question: What is 0?
Answer: One that is less than one
Question: Why the sun is not seen during the night?
Answer: Because it is afraid of the moon

Question: In that case why moon is seen only during the night?
Answer: Because it is not afraid of night
Question: What is the difference between Gandhiji and Netaji?
Answer: Gandhiji was a Neta but Netaji was not a Gandhi
Question: Sum up Income tax and GST
Answer: Income tax is good for Central Govt... Everything is good for GST.
Question: Who is an innocent and who is an Accountant?
Answer: Innocent is open and reveals the truth. An accountant is an open secret and creates the truth.

Thought
Smile to Smile

If a person keeps smiling all the time, then the genuineness of their smile Is questionable!
If a person keeps a sad and low face all day, however high his energy, It is deplorable!
If a person pursues his passion regularly, it is admirable!
If a person keeps chattering, unmindful of others' times, his chattering is Condemnable!
If a person remains in solitude for some time every day, it is commendable!
If a person brings a smile to a poor chap, his act is divinely adorable!

Humour
Fabulous Friday Medi (sin)

If you are perfectly all right, no need for any medicine
If you have a light headache you need only an Anacin
If you have a fever and headache then go for Metacin
If you want to feel relaxed use a sofa made of Rexine
If you want to feel intoxicated smell petrol or kerosene
If you want a lousy companion call your nearby cousin
If you want hygiene ask him to sanitize the washbasin!

Thought
Less luggage more space

When a house that was occupied for a long time is vacated, it becomes empty with all the belongings removed from the house. After such removal and cleaning, the house looks much bigger and more spacious than what it used to appear while it had people and belongings inside. We know that the space inside the house was the same both before occupation and after vacation. But the removal of goods and exit by the inmates of the house makes it possible to find more space inside the house.

Our minds are akin to the house. With the storage of multiple thoughts and incidents and their emotions, the quality space in the mind shrinks and stinks when thoughts are negative and depressing. Then, it suffocates more. But it becomes broad and spacious if it is cleansed up by removing every unnecessary thought and incident, especially the negative ones. In such a state, it will blossom, with a sweet fragrance and cheerful disposition. Why not cleanse the mind as often and allow it to remain open, if not to the sky, but at least to the soul?

Thought
Nothing to Nothing

We have surfaced in this world out of nothing, with a desire for one or another thing. Basic needs like food, clothes, and shelter are one thing; besides these, there is greed for many things. For money and power, we do anything. Success and fame are significant things; nothing short of craving in everything; every damn thing and our bodies will die; when we die, what remains? Nothing; who cares? None. We all are born and die for the sake of nothing!

Thought
My daily partners

Consciousness is my first life- partner;
Awareness is my all-time companion;
Love and compassion are my two eyes;
Experience is forever my best teacher;
Silence is my big contributing partner;
Smile is my daily intake of vitamin pills;
Humour is my boss who drills me, daily;
Boldness and courage are my caretakers;
Food and sleep are my life's pacemaker;

Money and friends are my well-wishers;
Introspection is my official supervisor;
Meditation is my only guide and master!

Humour

Alfred Einstein was a great scientist, me a sweet humourist!
Bernard Shaw was a brilliant man of wisdom and satire, I am a man of freedom who doesn't retire!
Charlie Chaplin was an impeccable silent comedian, me a charitable resilient Indian!
Donald Bradman was the greatest cricket legend, me an earnest producer of humour detergent!
Edmund Hillary was the first mountaineer to scale Everest, me the vibrant male who scaled Mt.Abu while taking a rest!
Florence Nightingale was the 'The lady with a lamp', me a laddy with frequent cramps, who sleeps in a night lamp!
George along with Washington was the first president of the US, and me, Joyram the first and last attendant in my home!
Hussein Bolt was the fastest sprinter, me the latest to attest that he is the fastest!
Issac Newton saw an apple falling and defined laws of motion, me seeing values falling, attribute it to the lack of devotion!

Thought
Education is God

Education powers knowledge
Knowledge empowers power
Power commands respect

Respect demands humility
Humility breeds an egoless mind
Egoless mind dwells in love
Love cascades into compassion
Compassion is the supreme human trait
Such a human is an envoy of God!

Thought
Empty vessel

We say that empty vessels make noise. When it comes to mind, the mind too is an empty vessel, when it was born. But over time, it starts making noises of all sorts, from little scratching sounds, to big banging. This happens when the mind is jittery, worried, afraid, confused, and bombarded by feelings of insult, loss of hope, determination, and courage. It also produces light and sweet musical sounds whenever one is in a good, positive, and pleasant mood. The mind vessel remains more silent when one thinks least, which is the last thing a mind can do.

One workable solution to keep the mind in a state of least noise and sweet noise is to observe it with all attention and deep awareness. To do this is like climbing Everest. It takes time, months, and years. In the case of Everest, one hoists the flag on reaching the summit. But in the case of conquering one's thoughts, hoisting colourful flags and deriving the joy of doing so is possible at every stage.

You initially observe your breathing so closely that you skip thinking during that time. This is the first occasion to hoist your first victory flag. Later you observe your thoughts in such a way that you look into them as an observer without getting entangled with them. If one could do this, even for a while, the second victory flag can be hoisted and the delight felt.

Moving further, one must resolve to muster all the boldness and courage, mentally, to thwart the tidal waves of coming and going worries, fears of the past, and the blinking of uncertainty by the future. Carrying on with this practice, one would soon find managing thoughts a little bit easier. If that happens, hoist yet another flag of success. But one should have the patience and perseverance to start afresh the entire above process, whenever one falls from the heights of advancement back to basics square one. More than any other visible life project, 'Project Mind Control' calls for the highest order of patience and perseverance.

By doing the above, one regulates one's mind vessel to resound and resonate more soothing and enjoyable tunes and arrest the scary, unpleasant, weird, and jarring tunes that the mind vessel is more capable of producing at any point in time.

So, what do you propose to do with your mind vessel?

Humour

A teacher blasted the principal of his school for not coming to the school in time. The principal remained calm and silent. The teacher is the father-in-law of the principal.

* * *

A class teacher has been suspended for one day for snoring in class while the District school education inspector was lecturing the students about the need for good sleep.

* * *

The history of a school teacher, who taught geography in English, had a mathematical brain that was triggered due to his chemistry with physics and his biological interest in social science.

* * *

Four students went late to the class. The teacher asked the students "Why are you late?"
First: I missed the train
Second: I missed the bus
Third: I missed the auto
Fourth: I missed all the three
Teacher???

* * *

The teacher announced in the class: "For the first time in the history of our school, there will be a sleeping competition for all the boys sitting on the last benches. For this competition, I have been shortlisted to take a class on "How to solve mathematical problems by using the brain" for one hour, for all the participating backbench students. The prizes will be under the 'quickest sleeper' and 'long sleeper' categories. To cheer up the sleeping students, our principal will also participate with the last bench students as a symbolic gesture.

* * *

In view of the revolutionary distance education program initiated by the government, the students of 'Faraway School' nearly cover a distance of 200 km daily. Initially, they travel 20 km to learn English. After that, they travel 30 km to attend Mathematics. From there they travel 40kms to hear from their science teacher. Soon they travel another 50kms to know about

History. To wind up the day, the students travel their last leg of 60 km and reach the PT (Physical Training) campus by 8 PM. Because they are already PT (physically tired) immediately they eat their dinner and go to sleep so that they can travel 200 more km the next day.

* * *

It was noon, there was no moon and it was a boon that I had no classes. Soon I entered the canteen and enjoyed my lunch with an attractive spoon, unmindful of a goon making fun of me. Later I went to my home and watched a cartoon of a buffoon playing with a big balloon. Gone are those days when I used to enjoy cone ice creams even at the cost of spoiling my tone, what to say, I even took a small loan to buy cone ice creams for which some of my friends called me a loon. But I don't mind even being called a poon. Still, I will be of my own even if I happened to live alone.

Thought
Nature vs. Humans

The colours of nature cannot be created artificially;
The rose flowers can't be rolled out of a machine;
The flowing stream of a river can't be duplicated;
The beauty of tidal waves is not for any copyright;
The physique of air can't be detected with an X-ray;
The creator of this universe cannot be CT-scanned;
That is the elegancy efficiency and truth of nature;
We can challenge nature but can never win over it!

Humour

Patient (inside the ambulance): The oxygen supply has stopped. Please arrange another refill immediately
Driver: The ambulance has stopped too. Please arrange another ambulance.

* * *

Patient's wife: Doctor, he faints every time whenever I serve him food.
Doctor: Then why don't you ask your husband to prepare the food?
Patient's wife: He only prepares the food, I just serve him.
The doctor faints...

* * *

Doctor: I can't give any guarantee about your husband's survival after the operation.
Patient's wife: Then what guarantee would you give?
Doctor: we two will survive.

* * *

Patient: when I touched you yesterday night, you didn't mind. But today you are not allowing me to touch you.
Nurse: That was my sister
Patient???

* * *

Patient: Nurse, till yesterday you gave me only one sleeping pill. Why are you administering two pills tonight?
Nurse: The pharma company has launched a special offer for their sleeping pills. 'Buy one, get one free" for the next month.
Patient???

* * *

Patient: Doctor, I am unable to eat.
Doctor: It is good, you save money, you know.
Patient???

* * *

Doctor: What happened, your front tooth is gone.
Patient: For telling the truth I lost my tooth.
Doctor???

* * *

Nurse: It is already 12 o clock at midnight. Why don't you sleep?
Patient: I am waiting for a female to join with me.
Nurse: One has to be married for that, you know.
Patient: Nurse, you are married, I know.

* * *

Doctor: I have already operated on your heart five times in the last five years. What is wrong?
Patient: Nothing wrong Doctor. Only my bank account has eroded to NIL balance.
Doctor???

* * *

Patient: With your best loving, affectionate, heart-touching, tender services in the last
Week, I feel robust, energetic, and fully charged now. So what is the next move?
Nurse: You will be discharged by tomorrow

* * *

Doctor: You are laughing at everything I say, what should I infer?
Patient: You are a good joker.
Doctor???

Thought
What catches up?

Gay abundance catches up during childhood!
Innocence catches up during initial school days!
Comparison catches up during the high school days!
Romantic sense catches up during college days!
Exhibition of knowledge catches up while seeking employment!
Asserting one's skills for reward catches up during employment!
Flaunting social stature catches up during post-marriage days!
During these times, the ego's influence catches up every day!
Ego, fully ripe disguised as maturity, catches up in the sixties!
More illness and less wellness catch up during the grey days!
A sort of realization catches up during the final phase of life!

Humour

I went to a shopping mall. I went to a branded wristwatch shop. I chose a particular model and asked "What is its price?" The salesman told, "Just wear it on your wrist, then the price will light up on the watch." I wore the watch. It lit up with the price "90.56 US dollars". I asked him "I am buying this watch in India, why the price is indicated in US dollars?" He replied, "Sir, this watch is manufactured in Zurich in limited numbers and is sold with dynamic pricing." Since I admired the watch, I bought it and wore it instantly on my hand. When I reached the billing counter, the billing clerk asked me to touch my wristwatch which I did. This time the price lit up was 120.98 UK pounds. Shocked, I promptly removed the watch, returned it to the sales counter, and told "If this is the case, I am not sure about the time it is going to show. It could be American or European or African time but not Indian time. I better go for Tata's Titan watch that comes with the Indian price and shows only Indian time."

Thought
Life is full of associations

Associations with people happen almost every day. But the majority of such associations wane out, with the completion of the purpose of such interim arrangements. Any commercial transaction is an apt example.

Almost fifty per cent of the remaining associations can be related to associations with relatives. Again, ninety per cent of such associations stand more as a formality. We meet relatives, only rarely, during events like marriage, etc. See, smile, greet, enquire, chat, dine, and part is the modus operandi, in general.

Ultimately special associations trickle down to the handful of ties with friends and relatives. Some of such associations with friends, shine like the bright stars in the night sky and sparkle like the colourful crackers lit during festivals. The personal meetings with them might be occasional, but the energy of mutual understanding, the excitement of spending a short time, even a few hours with them, and the enthusiasm triggered during the conversations uplift the spirit of the people involved.

Every person and every family blessed with such associations of friendship draws immense satisfaction and contentment of delight for having such great associations.

I am sure, you too must be part of such joy-triggering ties.

Thought
Life is like a tailor-made pants dress

It could be a pair of pants or a shirt. It could be formal or occasional wear. Most of the time, the stitched dress suits us Ok but not entirely to our satisfaction. Sometimes, the stitched clothes suit more perfectly, sometimes not so, mainly due to changes in our waist size and shape. The tailor too contributes to a comfortable fitting with his skilful cutting and stitching and at times, damages the dress as well, due to poor-quality stitching. At times, they need to be altered for a better fitting. Nevertheless, the stitched clothes are worn, anyway.

We too hand over ourselves to our mind-tailor, consciously or unconsciously. We live, enjoy, and suffer according to the quality of thoughts churned out by our mind cum master cum tailor. The experienced and expert tailors achieve more consistency of quality.

I wish you possess a good tailor in you.

Thought
The intentions matter

Eating for survival is not selfish but surviving on other's money is

Dressing for decency is not lavish but dressing just to show off is

Living in a big house is not atrocious but building it by cheating is

Taking help is not self-centric but taking always, without giving is

Spending a little time for chat is no waste, but daylong chatting is
Tasting a variety of foodstuffs is not a crime but wasting food is
Greeting without expectation is not cunning but with agenda, it is
Scolding someone by itself is not a bad act but with bad intentions is
Neglecting someone is not ungrateful but neglecting a best friend is

Humour

1. If the Taj Mahal was not built, there would not have been Taj hotels today!
2. The United States remains so due to the disintegration of people from their motherland!
3. If the moon didn't exist, scores of poets would have been shown the exit!
4. Minority rules the world, protecting their own interests, While the majority rules, paying them (minority) interests!
5. If pizza was not discovered, many with obesity would have recovered!
6. If I were not born, Joyram would have remained airborne!

Thought
Nothing like

Nothing like having a memorable childhood of play and fun;
Nothing like enjoying the days of carefree college life with friends;
Nothing like securing employment of our choice;
Nothing like a romance that continues post-marriage;
Nothing like contributing something to a social cause;
Nothing like extending a helping hand to the economically poor;
Nothing like keeping good holistic health and of cheerful disposition;
Nothing like practicing a hobby or two that refreshes renews energy, and rejuvenates us;
Nothing of the above can match, having an uninterrupted peaceful sleep that makes us feel the day like the beginning of a fresh life!

Humour
In a school

Teacher: What's your name?
Student: It's there on my birth certificate
Teacher: What you will study if you can't even tell your name?
Student: That I can't tell right now.
Teacher: I want to talk to your mother.
Student: She is in the car, chatting on WhatsApp with her students.

Teacher: Tell her to speak to me after the chat.
Student: I have already messaged her. She responded with a thumbs up.
Teacher: I want discipline first
Student: I want the helpline first
Teacher: The way you speak suggests that you could be the son of some VIP politician.
Student: No, not at all. For my UKG admission to this school, the capitation fee of Rs.3 lakhs itself is adequate to have a free-wheeling dialogue. By the way here is my promotion card at LKG in my earlier school.
Student: By the way, I forgot to ask your name.
Teacher: Your UKG class teacher, Mr Nambiyar
Student???

Thought
We live without realizing

Realities of life may be, except for the realization of mysterious Truth, must be faced, One day or the other, whether one likes it or not. Some of them are conflicts with one's principles and values, challenges posed by the social and economic anomaly, accounting for ethical and moral adherence, and facing the charges leveled by the consciousness through its agitations and upheavals.
Without realizing that we would soon pop out into this ridiculous world, we shrunk and expanded in our mother's womb for nine months!
Without any idea of how we were going to shape up, we went through an innocent childhood, oblivious to the environment surrounding us!

Without any intuition of what would be our career and profession, we were processed through schooling and college, thereby squeezing the experiences, reaped in the process!
Without exploring and realizing the potential of married life, we picked up a life partner through a horoscope or by choosing!
Without knowing the real purpose of giving birth, we yielded to our natural instincts and produced joint products, i.e. children, through time-bound joint ventures!
Without appreciating anything beyond the materialistic life, experiencing the innumerous joys and sufferings, in every walk of life, we invariably board the special coach, detached from the mainstream life train!
Without achieving a perfect 10 in life, without any exception, without knowing what to do next, we await the next move by destiny, keeping our fingers crossed!

Thought
Twenty-two turned, and twenty-three now tuned

When every New Year arrives, greet us, the passing calendar year does puzzle us. Welcoming New Year is a worldwide ritual. It also prompts for any left-over's renewal. Now is the time to roar in joy and reverberate. It is crucial to introspect and self-interrogate. 2022 brought us smiles, and tears good and bad. Let's leave the past, not feeling bad or sad. Taking the points from past gains and pains. We can chart a viable map for certain wins. The ringing of the 2023 bell will spread joy threads. New Year will also have its quota of threats. Appreciating these, let's sing and dance together.

Humour
The Corporate personalities

A CEO stands for Costliest Expenditure Object.

A GM stands for Great Miss-manager.

An executive is one who has already worked with an ex-employer, generally cute but not productive.

An Accountant is one who counts in foreign currency, accounts in local currency, and discloses the end result like that of an elephant, both in words and figures.

A supervisor is super and wiser and eats his supper but not like his superior, whose supper is superior to the supervisor due to the addition of soup.

An assistant is one who works like an ass (donkey) and is made to sit in the distance like a distant relative.

An attendant is one who is at times tender and renders services that are generally redundant.

A watchman is a person who watches every man moving around, even if there is no man.

A Security person is one who secures a secured telephone line with the office secretary.

Thought
When one stays in these countries

US, one makes so much of a fuss
British, one lives cold and peevish
Russia, one can't see a messiah
China, one will stare at Corona
Germany, life will be in harmony
India, life is sunny yet with a platter of honey!

Thought
Organ donation

When people are scared to part with even their nails!
There exists a breed of brave-hearts telling tales!
Be it the eye, heart, kidney, or liver, they forego with guts!
We find more of such champions in the streets and huts!

Humour
Laugh or weep

1. Who is the tallest person in the world?

The one who is taller than the second tallest person.

2. Who built the Taj Mahal?

Even Shahjahan himself didn't know when someone asked him "Who built it?"

3. What is the difference between Sun and Petrol?

Sun is concerned with the rise; Petrol is concerned with price.

4. What is the similarity between sun and petrol prices?

Both rise daily, invariably.

5. When the tidal waves in the oceans will cease?

When the human mind stops thinking.

6. Will God rescue this, dangerously spoiled world?

This question is unwarranted when the real concern is "Who will rescue God from the clutches of human beings"?

7. Why does the sun vanish at night?

Human beings would exploit it by tapping more solar ENE, by doing overtime and threatening en sun's existence.

8. What comes after one?

One that goes after one.

Thought
Life is uncertain

Life inside the womb is uncertain
Uncertain life after birth is certain
It's certain that the future is uncertain
The past is certain behind the curtain
The present too is not so certain
The future is of course uncertain
Certain are certain uncertainties
Uncertain the beginning certainly
Certain end is uncertainly certain!

Thought
Nothing but everything

The world today is at its peak of intelligence
Scientists showcase it with over-confidence
God's physical existence is yet to be proven
Atheists are upbeat, claiming they have won
Humans' creation is a pointer to ponder over
The origin that created us remains a wonder
Inertiartia that existed before the big banging
Must have been the void space in the Kingkong?
This theory implies that 'nothing is everything'
God must be nothing, God is also everything
Now redefining everything is nothing but God
It is absurd to depict God as one with a word!

Thought
Expect, Except, Exempt

Life is nothing but expectations and exceptions
What one doesn't expect occurs as an exemption
For people's expectations, there is no exception
Exception can't be exempted even for expected
Expecting no expectations is very rarely exempt
Expected exemptions are, therefore exceptions!

Thought
I am one who is no one

I am a teacher who never teaches any students
I am a lawyer who has neither choice nor a voice
I am a doctor who practices without medication
I am an Engineer who sketches all shiny hitches
I am a pilot who owns a plane that can't take off
I am a poet whose poems are yet to be scripted
I am a humourist who weeps for his fans to laugh
I am a cop who holds a gun but can't find a thief
I am an Accountant, tallying suspense accounts
I am an entertainer whose audience never exist!

Thought
Two birthdays, why not?

I was born on this date, as the nth-child, adding to my big family kitty. Later, at age 6, I was enrolled in a school, as an additional boy in the first standard. Subsequently, I was roped into another primary school, into the second standard, as an extra but ordinary student. Years rolled by, my physique growing up, eyes looking up, the objects and people (whenever they didn't watch me), my mind becoming more and more disorderly and restless.

When I was 17 years, my parents realized that my horoscope was cast wrongly. Instead of 17th April, the original date of birth, the horoscope was cast based on 17th May as my birth date. For school records, nothing could be done, at that stage and so I remained to date, as was born on 17th May only. But my horoscope was recast when I was 17 which drew a picture of glow and gloom about my future. It predicted that I was going to be a short-tempered guy, with a passion for certain arts and fine arts. The document also clarified that I would end up, not as an artist but as a diehard public servant, for earning my bread and butter.

Today, I am wondering in awe, at this prediction made that day. I retired after serving in a PSU for 35 years; to date, I continue to draw my own unknown fans, which good or bad seem to like my style of singing in the online singing apps. The horoscope analysis proved more or less correct with its branding of me as a short-tempered person. This remains to date as a matter of fact. On this day of my duplicate birthday, that paved way for ascertaining my originality, at a later date, I feel pride for having been bestowed with the opportunity of celebrating two birthdays every year, not to talk about cutting cakes or sorry figures.

Thought
Fall in all

All are thinkers but many are with blinkers;
All have some skills but only a few will;
All have compassion but mostly with ration;
All possess arts but only a few touch hearts;
All perceive matters but only some matters;
All play indoor games few only play outdoors;
All have expertise but smart ones advertise;
All like success but limited few have access;

All want money but the rich only has it many;
All want everything while joy needs nothing;
All want to be in a joyful state but not the joy!

Thought
The best and the worst about life

The best thing about life is, one can choose
The worst thing about life is, its certain woos
Life's bonus is, living amidst beautiful nature
The onus is on people to carve the signature
The mystery of life unfolds during self-inquiry
The poetry of gloom is life's inevitable theory
The great boon is, no curbs on one's thinking
The tricky fact is, no signs that one is sinking
The evil spirit, money hurts moneyless dearly
Money monster paints even thieves gloriously!

Thought
Respect and emotions

It is not only strange but ironic that we meet some persons in our life, only to engage in verbal altercations and battles. Such a person may be anything, from a beggar to even, a saintly figure. I had such kind of one-off peculiar verbal fight, even with a fake self-proclaimed saint. Whether the opposite party is a beggar or pious saint, respect is to be given first, to the other party. Respect cannot be demanded or commanded but is reserved and served only to the deserved. During my service in an organization, spanning over thirty-five years, I had one such altercation with my senior executive that was witnessed not only by my section but the entire department. I shouted at the height of my voice. I had scolded my immediate boss and almost tarnished his image in the process. That fight I had with him, was something like a foundation of the sort and paved the way for my aggravated and aggressive reaction with some other people in my life, who happens to be my best friends, to date. That day my officer did not respect me and as a consequence earned the dirtiest of my ire and anger. This incident was never a joyful one but on the other hand one of the most horrible experiences in my life because that incident also exhibited my immaturity, my emotion, and my weakness in being ill-treated by the other person.

Thought
A to F

After adequate analysis of alternatives act appropriately
Behold your breath, build bravery, and bloom beautifully
Care, crave, crack, and create a colourful catchy canopy
Dare, do, dismantle, and destroy, disturbing dirty devils
Energize, engage, endure, empower, and evaluate daily
Fuel freedom, fight fatigue, flow flawlessly, and feel fine!

Humour

Rarely when others manipulate me as bait I don't hate them but bate!
I have one enemy, and it is fate, which I realized last night rather late!
As a bachelor, I wore a coat, lay on a single cot, lacking a roommate!
I can eat ten bars of chocolate only if they are served on a golden plate!
After reading this if you still feel normal you are really great!

Thought
Summer is hot but mangoes are sweet

Posting a motivational message is as good as child's play! Telling advice to people who seek it, is like sleeping in a luxury cot! Admiring others' excellence is like a train passing through a station!
Abundant laughter is like a gift, bestowed for the art of spontaneous humour!
A life without failures, problems, and sorrows is like the ice cubes formed during freezing winter!
A life of constant and multiple perils that steal seize and seal one's joy, is like a mango tree that bears only decayed and spoiled mangoes! A child playing merrily in the cosy of his home, avoiding summer, won't get a variety of gifts from others during summer holidays, but instead will get fed up with crates of ice cream in the biting cold, unable to enjoy the ripe and delicious mangoes available only during summer.

Thought
Every person is a continent

Every person is as unique as a continent; Like, the countries in a continent has similarities in climate, race, tradition, culture etc, every individual has their own physiological biological as well as psychological pockets inside, complicately knit closely; Some faculties in a person thrives, some fail, some breaks down, some gets rusted and some arrested within; Like the US prospering at the cost of other countries, like China dumping its infinite gadgets in other countries, like ndia accommodating and tolerating the best and worst practices of every section of its people, in the name of whatever one may call; like British over-ruling other countries for centuries and now being overruled, overlooked and overshadowed in this century; like the erstwhile USSR integrated by a common language and the, then prevailing corporeal power of communism, now disintegrated into as many countries; Such two distinct, disintegrated countries Russia and Ukraine, with many similarities in race, culture and tradition, are now fighting among themselves, inciting even remote possibilities of another global war.

Some people are like Africa (more darkness less light), some are like Australia (more space with lesser people) and some like Antarctica (freezing and biting, not living-friendly), just to mention the traits and characteristics of a few people.

Thought
The world of the middle class

This world is full of puzzles and surprises, in addition to the ever-remaining suspense about the existence or absence of God. On the one side, we find teeming millions grinding in utter poverty and on the other side we find lakhs of people rolling on wealth, falling and stumbling on prosperity. In between these two lopsided divisions, we have the impeccable roly-poly toys-like people, called the middle class. The middle class is one that is poised in such a way that it could either claim to have little access over the wealthy class or compare itself to the poor class, depending on the circumstances. They are the footballs that take the kicks and beats from the other people of two extreme classes. These people are generally classified as employees who are supposed to lead a decent life. They find it difficult to save money but have to save to sustain as middle class to survive so n the long run. Even after paying a big cut of their income as taxes, they are not expected to become poor.

Thought
What is this destiny?

A man, born in a hut, flies his own personal jet! Another one, born with a silver spoon, later becomes a circus buffoon!
Yet another, dumped as one among ten siblings, turns into an expert on family planning! Some, born into a wealthy family, one day, fall into a poverty ditch!

A few, produced in a filthy and flimsy slum, go on to churn prosperity and turn fatty sum!

Not everyone becomes a scholar, an employer, a politician, an artist, a scientist, an industrialist, a businessman, and a celebrity, a player of success, reputation, and admiration!

There is something called DESTINY, that decisively and unilaterally directs every creature's course of life. It is defined and described in as many terms. Fate, fortune, hard work, luck, intelligence, intellect, and good or bad time, are some of them. Who directs this invisible yet invincible destiny that is the root cause of every commotion in this world?

Of course, each one of us.

Thought
Breathe to more happiness

The ultimate goal of everyone in life is happiness; but, happiness is both at the surface and deep levels; raw satisfaction is derived by enjoying pleasures; each pleasure is momentarily borne out of the senses; these sensual pleasures only hurt pain later; mere indulging in pleasures won't give happiness.

To arrest this vicious cycle of pain to gain one needs to feel happiness of the higher order. Is that possible? Yes, it is possible to realize more qualitative and authentic happiness.

The ways are many that can be followed. One of the best methods, explored, experienced, practised, and more often realized by people of both ordinary and extraordinary traits, is observing oneself in silence. You may call it meditation, inspection, introspection, etc. I am not any author or authority to prescribe any methods or school of thought. I am just sharing my tailor-made way of practising meditation. Only those who feel comfortable with this, after reasonable practice, may wish to carry on with this method, if one likes it.

About the methodology
All that you need is to sit in silence, preferably in solitude. It is better if the environment is serene. Sitting in a comfortable position, on the floor or chair, back resting more erect, with eyes closed. There are no hard and fast rules about the duration of this meditation. Start by observing your breathing completely, when you inhale and exhale the air. It is not an easy job, at least for beginners. Spending five to ten minutes, in the beginning, is fine.
Later on, one can increase the time according to one's comfort level. Even while inhaling and exhaling your mind will wander about in its usual not-yielding ways but as you start focusing on your breathing, there will be little pauses and little pockets of no-thought moments in your mind, during this practice.
But this practice, cannot guarantee one 24/7 happiness. Because, as long as one treads in the path of material life, it is impossible to achieve happiness at every moment.

Humour

I got into my car and started it. It didn't start.
I came out, to look for some help. But there was no one.

I called my home but no one answered.
I rushed to security, but could not find one.
I looked at my watch, but it showed the time on Mars.
I started walking but could not find any path.
I started breathing but could not find my lungs.
I felt like I was dying but destiny was not nearby.
I started crying loudly and found my spouse murmuring to herself
"When are you going to stop screaming while dreaming"?

* * *

Thought
Remembering the vital importance of total health

Health is wealth, wealth without health life is a myth; at a young age we are taught about moral values and discipline; but never about the importance of health; in the next stage were we told about physical health.

Mental health was not given much significance; when we matured into a more complete Persons, we discovered or heard that health means holistic health; over the ages, self-conscious people cared for total health; today, the deaths due to reasons of carelessness and negligence are more than deaths caused by killer diseases like cancer, strokes, respiratory illness, etc.

The current and past generations have started to realize and appreciate the impact of one's health in their life, both career and personal life; with these in the backdrop, many champions have brought awareness to the public about the importance of practising yoga for an active, energetic, stress-free life. Yoga can be used to promote mental health, thereby striking an optimum balance between body and mind.

If Patanjali was the pioneer in spreading yoga, yogic gurus like Tirumalai Krishnamacharya, Sivananda, Swami Rama, and B.K.S.Iyengar contributed immensely to the furtherance of holistic yogic practices for the common man. It would be a mistake if one doesn't recognize the great yogic services of the yogic trainer, Ramdev Ji. In fact, it is Ramdev ji who took yoga to the grass root levels across India. He deserves great admiration, appreciation, and accolades for his contributions to promoting the physical well-being of crores of people in and around India. India has made the entire world recognize the role of yoga in people's overall well-being by making the UN declare the 21st of June every year, as world yoga day.

Every individual would be immensely benefited, if he or she could practice any of the authenticated and proven yogic practices, on a regular basis. I can vouch that my little yoga practice has bestowed me with better health and mind. Let us join hands in promoting Yoga in our homes, and neighbourhoods and contribute a little good to our society.

Yoga triggers health; Health promotes happiness: Happiness brings peace.

Thought
Nothing happens without something

Nothing is available without it getting charged first!
The cellphone is usable only when its battery is charged!
Food is available only against payment of the food bill!
Romantic love is possible only when two hearts are mutually charged!
Remuneration is made only against services rendered to an employer!
Anger on others is vented because of the anger one has with oneself!
Friendly chat is possible only when friends are charged with positive vibes!
WhatsApp messages happen because two people's mind is charged mutually!
A crime is charge-sheeted while a noble deed is appreciated!
Hence nothing happens without something happening!

Thought
We feel we know everything, without knowing anything

We enter into this world without knowing so!
We grow into adults without trying to be so!
We become something without realizing so!
We indulge in nonsense without understanding so!
We train to drain ourselves without appreciating so!

We reward ourselves with false ego without thinking so!
We punish ourselves with our habits without minding so!
We become ordinary followers without discovering so!
We focus mainly, on filling the belly without observing so!
We hide realities in the name of status without feeling so!
We end up, living worthless life without accepting so!
We finally evaporate as nothing, without knowing so!

Thought
A good day

A good day doesn't end as such but by beginning so. That doesn't happen by itself but with the conscious efforts of oneself. Dawn with smiles and cheers is most likely the factor that signals a good day in the pipeline. One can't wake up with positive reflexes on their face and mind unless one posted a decent sleep the day before. Once this is ensured, it is the twin weapons in action ie attitude and behaviour that shapes and carves how the day would progress. The day would end up as good or bad accordingly.

A person who could achieve five good days in a week is surely a fine example of an excellent person who makes his/her life good.

Humour

Harmless Diwali eve crackers

Friend 1: I had a terrible dream yesterday, my wife thrashed me with a big cane stick.

Friend 2: Yours was only a dream. I had a horrible experience yesterday, my neighbour's wife chased me with a broomstick.
Friend 1: what went wrong?
Friend 2: I told her 'You look like a Joystick'.
Friend 1???

* * *

Patient: I vomit whatever I eat.
Doctor: Then omit to eat.
Patient???

* * *

Neighbour 1: Your dog barks all day, your cat keeps mewing during the night, and your wife keeps yelling at you all the time.
Neighbour 2: These are natural and common everywhere. What's your problem?
Neighbour 1: My tigress is afraid to come out of the house.
Neighbour 2: How dare could you grow a wild animal in a residential area?
Neighbour 1: I meant my wife.
Neighbour 2???

* * *

Thought

The ever-green but old debate

Man is an offshoot of God and nature. He is God, in as much as his abilities to create and procreate. He is natural to a tiny extent in his attitude to giving help and services to others.

Mankind conveniently forgot about its original identity because its grandparents and forefathers too didn't know that. God must be that super eternal power, which seldom takes birth anywhere beyond the boundaries of nothingness. This is just my inference and nothing else.

In the Mahabharat epic, Lord Krishna preached by emphasizing and reiterating the existence of a formless, birthless and deathless eternal, indestructible soul, which is the very life force in ourselves.

Buddha claimed to have attained enlightenment, but no one knew the truth of what he experienced and realized except his teaching that the state of 'Nil' balance in a person's Desire account, could lead to one's liberation.

Ramana Maharshi, we are told, deep dived within himself explored, and apparently tapped the door to 'Who am I'. But not even a single soul was really sure about his rendezvous with his own self. Everyone seemed to have deduced, derived and arrived at their self-believed conclusions that ever remain inconclusive.

Therefore, as far I am concerned, with the few droplets of my life experiences, the utter reality is the existence of our physical bodies, over the years we have been living with, their visible physical movements, and their never-ending mental waves of thoughts that sweep in astronomical speed. Their disguised curse is their ability to register, remember and recollect the incidents of the f past, so vividly, which is mostly to their disadvantage.

I am also convinced that there always exists, will exist, the concept of duality, both in the spheres of material and spiritual planes. If there can be a 'bad against a good and a plethora of such accompanying pairs of opposites, there must be a doctrine of the non-existence of God against. The school of thought God exists. There is not even an iota of doubt in me, that we are all but bundles of emotions in varying degrees, where feelings and passion are inseparable parts of emotion.

Believing in the existence of God, going to places of worship, and praying to God with helplessness and despair, happen because of the time-old conditioning of their minds (in the names of religion, customs, traditions, beliefs, etc) and nothing more than that.

The creation of God by man is mainly to overcome his fears of imminent death and his despair to prolong his survival for worldly pleasures.

History, now and in posterity as well, will have no definite authentic verifiable clue, whatsoever, regarding the never-ending cycle of births and deaths. The incident that happens between birth and death will remain as 'never resolved, everTamilry'.

I endorse and salute an adage in Tamil that means "Those who discovered it never tell and those who tell never discovered it".

Humour

Bernard Shaw was a king of his own in political satire and humour, although he was a great dramatist by profession. Sam Manekshaw was the great Field Marshal and chief of our army during the seventies when, under his command, Pakistan surrendered to India, and a new country Bangladesh was born. I thought of imagining a fantasy-like episode, involving these two Shaws. My imagination goes like this:

Bernard Show was writing a play for staging another drama. He thought of a strong and interesting character in his play that would make the audience sit erect throughout the play. He thought of many like Mussolini, Hitler, Alexander, Napoleon, Julius Caesar, and many such warriors and leaders but could not fit into the role he was imagining. Suddenly, it struck him "How about Indian army officer Manekshaw? At that time Sam was a young Indian colonel. A couple of years earlier, Manekshaw was recognized for his bravery and smart strategy when he led his regiment successfully in the Pagoda hills while fighting against the Japanese Imperial Army during world war 1942. In this encounter, he was badly wounded by multiple bullets. But he recovered dramatically. Bernard admired him after reading the news about this. He wondered "In spite of different careers in life, Manekshaw and I share certain similarities". He was right. Both names contained 'Shaw' in the end. Bernard Shaw was a polemicist, (one who engages in a controversial debate). Manekshaw, a brilliant military officer had a huge sense of humour and was controversial to some extent. He originally wanted to become a doctor but when his father declined his interest, Manekshaw, more out of a rebellious mood chose the army. Both wanted total freedom for giving their best.

Manekshaw fought wars, mostly outside India; Bernard Shaw fought many politicians and celebrities across the world, with his brilliant wisdom and knowledge which were soaked in wit and humour. Manekshaw held Bernard in high esteem and was his admirer. Bernard managed to establish contact with Manekshaw in India and requested him along with his wife to come to London to spend a few days with him. Luckily Manekshaw was preparing to avail a long holiday around that time. He gladly accepted Bernard's invitation and went to London where Bernard Shaw arranged decent accommodation in a hotel for Manekshaw and his wife. Manekshaw knew Bernard's simple lifestyle and asked him in a lighter vein "Sir, I am sure this hotel suit must have been arranged by one of your fans." Bernard replied in his impeccable style "Rather, I arranged for my fan to book you, this hotel accommodation". Although Manekshaw enjoyed the hotel suite, he could not spend much time going around because Bernard wanted to discuss with him at his home only, which was on par with an ordinary home. Manekshaw found another bottleneck, Bernard was a vegetarian. So he was forced to eat only vegetarian food in the company of Bernard. Manekshaw once quipped "Sir, I wish we were vegetarians". Bernard matched him instantly "Your wish is granted, you can go to India and tell the people "We were vegetarians in London". Manekshaw could not control his laugh.

Shaw inquired Manekshawabout his personal life. Manekshaw gave a detailed history of his past which Bernard listened to with keen ears. Bernard said, "While I make satire with my words of expressions you create impressions with your attire." Manekshaw laughed loudly. When Manekshaw asked Bernard "How come, Sir, with all such name and fame you continue to live a simple life?" for which Bernard said, "The reason is 'simple'". Manekshaw experienced another burst of laughter.

Bernard told him" Look, I am writing a play for my next stage drama and I have proposed a vital character in this play who will be more or less like you." Manekshaw asked, "How about its nose, will it be the same as mine, like the woodpeckers?" Then it was Bernard's turn to laugh. He said "Why not, we have many people here who are woodcutters by profession but politicians by confusion." Manekshaw chuckled at this comment and said "Mahatma Gandhi has started 'Quit India movement; it is becoming tougher for the British to manage Indian people. I am confident that we will win our war of non-violence soon'. Bernard heard this and told, "What you tell the British in India, people tell me here often 'Quit England". But I won't quit England till such time Englishmen understand what is wit." This made Manekshaw giggle. Bernard quickly added, "Violence is good as long as it is without violence".

Bernard asked "You have not responded to me about my including your character in my next play"

Manekshaw replied "It will be my pleasure, Sir. I wonder how nice it would be if I were to enact that character myself in the play." Bernard responded naughtily "In that case, the audience would suspect, going by your name, that I have one more beloved and my offspring in India, the country, which I have not visited so far." Manekshaw threw his heavy wit-weight and said " But your Indian beloved could always visit you here, isn't it Sir? Bernard literally hit Manekshaw at this and laughed uncontrollably.

Bernard thanked Manekshaw for giving his consent to include his character in his next play. He wished him "All the best in your future military endeavours and all the best for India to become an independent nation at the earliest. Convery my personal regards to Mahatma Gandhi, the child-like innocent leader". Manekshaw wished him "Thank you, Sure, Sir, I wish you more nobles and laurels, in the near future". Bernard in his unique manner said, “I don’t think that learned fools would think of a hardened fool for the second time and lose their hardly hard-earned money.

* * *

Thought
Your life is your garden

Wake up the smile in you every day;
Exercise your body, befriend your mind;
Resolve to be bold and courageous;
Greet, cheer up as many as you can;
Extend even little help to the needy;
Mind you, you are the best celebrity;
Whenever the past peeps just ignore;
Anything of the past is as good as dead;
Nobody stays with you but you only;
So no one gives you joy but you only!

Thought
The middle class is like middle birth

This is a chaotic world. To live here in total freedom is impossible. Even if you reach the forest, the lions and tigers will not spare you and your freedom. Even if you climb the Himalayas, there would be your predecessors roaming, sitting, chatting, meditating, and going there with the objective of having total freedom, exactly in tandem with your objective. These acts sound more like spiritual endeavours. Such people are the negligible least.

There is another elated minority group of people, those literally rolling on wealth. These people have their plans cut out for enjoying life to their satisfaction. Not only Money is no constraint for them, but almost nothing is a constraint for them. Their only constraint may be their incapacity to enjoy whatever they hear and see due to health and other such issues. They board the richest airlines; they cruise on ultra-modern luxurious ships, they champagne with the oldest and most authenticate alcohol available in the world.

Those falling between the above two extreme categories are the poor and the poor like middle-class people. Utterly poor sleep with little food or no food. The middle class can't sleep without food. They can't remain without feeling the pinch of having less money. They can't remain idle without working for more money. Their wants climb up steadily in proportion to their earnings but eventually, their wants would take the driver's seat without really being driven. The middle class suffers terribly, struggles continuously, takes beatings, and looks to others to console themselves or to work hard for better standards.

They can't stoop down to low levels nor behave like loyal servants to their masters. They have every stuff of knowledge and ability and enough of everything except the blessings of lady luck, ie enough money. They plan occasionally for renouncing life but life never renounces them.

Humour

This morning I noticed the switch for the geyser in the bathroom was loose and shaky. But somehow I managed to switch on the geyser. My geyser is noise friendly. But to my shock, I heard an unusual noise from operating the small machine. I immediately pointed to my wife who was surprised by my complaint. She went and checked the switchboard and did something, the noise completely stopped. She turned and told me "Along with the geyser's switch you switched on the exhaust fan's switch as well". I made a clumsy smile at my wife and proceeded to take my bath, without making any noise, whatsoever.

Thought
'A' to 'O'

Aspire Abundantly
Brave Bottlenecks
Create Confidence
Develop Dexterity
Execute Earnestly
Finish Faultlessly
Garner Garlands
Help Helpless
Introspect Inwards
Joke Joyfully
Knit Knowledge
Learn Lavishly

Move Majestically
Narrate Nicely
Oh! Outstanding!

Thought
Think productively Talk purposefully

Talking without any stuff is a hobby!
Talking to the point is a skill!
Eating for enjoyment is a habit!
Eating for happiness is an art!
Outside knowledge is a liability!
Understanding this is an asset!
Doing duty is for earning a living!
Earning life honours is real earning!
Thinking unnecessary is normal
Thinking to promote joy is wisdom!
Running for the race is drilling!
Running in the race is thrilling!
Who are my dream girl and darling?
Every bird that I let go to Darjeeling!

Thought
Clueless life

Endless thinking, aimless efforts, goalless life, careless love, penniless charity, salt-less food, meaningless friendships, witless conversations, pointless discussions, needless advice, reckless driving, regardless etiquette, compassion-less attitude, heartless behaviour, flavour-less tea, tasteless sweet, waterless watermelon, hot less soup, and more of these less, make one's living baseless, worthless and leads to a charmless life that is nothing less than hopeless, which makes life, more or less, lifeless. Are these words meaningless?

* * * * *

Humour
Cubits

The best place to eat is in a relative's marriage. One pays for one day (gift) and eats for three days.

Don't think that only the dogs on the streets bark at you. Many dogs from inside the houses bark. More furiously, either with or without the "Beware of dogs" signboard outside.

In big gatherings the audience, when the speaker refers to some as fools, many look around just to ensure that others don't look at them.

If you successfully fail to make it onto the stage, you would have succeeded in failing at that Stage.

Thought
The best and worst friend

A best friend is one who takes the worst from you and still runs to you to help and give his best when you are in distress; the worst friend is one who neglects and runs away from you, after taking the best from you.

Why are many of the apartments five-storied? Because if there are six floors, those living on the Sixth floor would be cursed with the sixth sense.

Thought
What lasts in our minds?

What lasts in our minds, is it one's words or deeds? Of course, deeds. Does it not make us pleasant whenever we help others? It is all the more heartening if we extend helping hands to the poor. We feel good to speak positive and kind words to others. How glad and satisfying it feels, to motivate others? It is sheer joy whenever we smile genuinely at others. Others' many helping acts may not stay ever in the mind. One's words of confidence, hope and faith, later on, we may not remember. A Plethora of smiles sent to us or sent to others doesn't get registered for long.

But one thing gets deeply etched in our memories. It is the way one behaves and interacts with us. We remember easily at any point in time how a person behaved with us.

Whenever you interact with people, ensure that those you interact with leave you, cheerfully, without leaving you. This is adequate for availing your quota of peace and happiness on any day.

Humour

The popular actress with some unpopular fans, Ms.MotiMotwani retired from active acting and called a press conference to inform her decision, which the entire film industry and cinemagoers were eagerly expecting.

Reporter 1: You claim your present age as 35 and have acted for more than 25 years. Did you start acting at ten?

Actress: Yes, my mother was an actress, having acted silently in more than fifty movies. My grandmother too was an actress of reckoning who spoke five to ten few words in those silent movies. But due to the curbs imposed by the then censor board, her words were muted. In fact, I began acting when I was just a three-year-old baby. But the producers and directors at that time never looked up to a ten-year-old girl for acting talents. That was not my fault.

Reporter 2: One of your ex-husbands informed us that you are actually 53 but claim yourself as 35 years old.

Actress: Don't get misled by ex-husbands and ex-wives. They never want their ex-spouses to be happy. When the number 9 could be interpreted as 6 by some blind people, my age is also read incorrectly by some naughty and haughty people. Never mind it. Let me tell you one thing. Age is just an illusion but what one looks like is the secret of their make-up solution.

Reporter 3: You claim you are not married. But your two ex-husbands claim that they got married to you.

Actress: Yes and No. I divorced both of them for their diversified activities with some classified actresses on vitrified as well as verified mattresses. Even a small child of two and a half years will tell that after divorcing your spouse, you once again become unmarried. Very true, isn't it?

Reporter 4: You reported that five films in which you acted as heroine ran for more than 100 days. But not even one movie was a box office hit. Please explain the paradox.
Actress: 19+11+ 34+ 17+ 29. Use both your brain as well as the cellphone calculator. Don't these add up to more than 100?
Reporter 5: It seems you told two of your neighbour that two producers, two directors, and two heroes cheated you on two occasions. Can you please elaborate on this two-liner in two to two sentences?
Actress: Two producers booked me as heroines for two movies but at the last minute changed my role as the villain in the same movie. That movie became a hit, was another story. But the world did not know that the hero of that film treated me as his heroine behind the movie.
Two directors exploited my beauty in their movies but subtracted my original beauty in acting. But ultimately eleven of my fans praised my outward beauty in that movie which gave some solace to me. Only the other naughty and fatty fans requested me to stop acting in movies.
Two heroes promised to take me to Nayagara Waterfall and the Taj Mahal but instead took me to Nigeria false water and Madurai Nayakar Mahal. But I was glad that no one noticed me both in Nigeria and Madurai except these two heroes who later became my husbands and ex-husbands, later.
Reporter 6: It seems you were offered the role of Kasthuri Bhai Gandhi but refused it at the last moment. Why?
Actress: My grandmother saw Mahatma Gandhi. My mother saw Kasthuri Bhai Gandhi. But I have not seen even Attenburrow's Gandhi. So how could I do justice to that role? But I gave them one option I was prepared to do the role of Mrs Rahul Gandhi. That was five years back but to date,

I didn't hear anything from the producers. Later some of my fans informed me that the producer left the film field once and for all.

* * *

Thought
Impressive, isn't it?

A person, who is aggressive in pursuing his objectives, never abusive of his opponents, and conducive and impassive in his behaviour, generally archives impressive results. If he is not evasive in his commitments, not regressive in his techniques, and submissive while putting across his thoughts, he gets massive support. Further, if he acts like an adhesive in uniting two opposing parties, is responsive whenever his attention or intervention is sought, and gives conclusive ideas that are inclusive, he will receive active cooperation from all around. If such a person is cohesive, in his communication and acts, even if being gently defensive and subtly offensive, he will make himself a progressive leader.

Quote

Appreciating the difficulties of life and others is called understanding!

Appreciating and accepting the problems we face is called maturity!

* * *

Humour
God visits New Delhi

God (disguised as a saint): Bhavathi Bhiksham Dehi. (Oh, noble Lady, please give some alms)
House wife: Kal aanaa. Rotiki chawal doongi. (Meaning, you come tomorrow. I shall give you Rice made from Roti)
God comes out banging the gate, murmuring "Saale, 'tu kanjoose marwari ki pathni ho'
(Meaning, 'you stupid wife of a miser')

* * *

God: (disguised as a student): I want to study the special course 'The many ways to reach Vaikundam"
Medical College official: We have a 'Vaikundam' vehicle for people's final journey parked in the garage and the only way to reach there is through the backyard. There is no need for any special course to reach Vaikundam.
However, if you are very keen on doing a special study, you may try our newly introduced course "Who is more reliable, a Surgeon or God?"
God instantly vanishes.

* * *

God (disguised as a devotee): I want to go inside the sanctum santorum and rest for the night.
Priest: "Are you a fool or what. Practically there is no air inside. There is no fan, no AC. Even if the real God comes and sleeps there, he will die. You cannot rest even for five minutes inside. Better sleep on the roadside platform where you will get some fresh air. But negotiating with the local mosquitoes is your lookout.

God disappears from the scene.

* * *

God asks at the 'Help desk": Is there a bus to 'Mount Kailash'?
Help Desk: Sorry. There is a bus to go to greater Kailash via Papi Dham. For reaching Mount Kailash, first of all, you must become a godly person and live in the deep forests of the Himalayas.
God: Of course, I am from the top of the Himalayas. Can't you even make out that I am a godly person?
Help Desk (laughing loudly): You look like a buffoon with such unimaginable costumes. Even God will not certify that you are a godly person. 'Tu sidemen khade hojavo. Tumhare peeche bahuth sarae log Papi dham Jane keliye ghadi number poochrahi hai'.
(Meaning, 'you better stand by the side. There are many commuters waiting behind, who want to know the bus number for travelling to Papi Dham')
In disillusionment, God finds himself on 'Mount Kailash', looking completely shattered, and crying to his better half "Mujhe ab dar lagraha hai ki ye paagal insaan log kabhi bhi Mount kailash poonchke hameybhi kabja kar sakte hai. Issey pehele hum khud yahan sey dafa hojayenge aur Vaikundam mein uttharenge. Wahan, tumhari bhai Vishnu ji ke sath kaisebhi adjust karke jeeyenge.
(Meaning 'I am afraid that these insane humans will soon reach Mount Kailash and capture us. Before that happens, let us disappear from this place and go to Vaikundam, where we will somehow adjust ourselves with your brother Vishnu and live').

* * *

Thought
More or less meaningless

Endless thinking, aimless efforts, goalless life, careless love, penniless charity, saltless food, meaningless friendships, witless conversations, pointless discussions, needless advice, reckless driving, regardless etiquette, compassion-less attitude, heartless behaviour, flavourless tea, tasteless sweet, waterless watermelon, hot less soup, and more of these less, make one's living baseless, worthless and leads to a charmless life that is nothing less than hopeless, which makes life, more or less, lifeless.

* * *

Humour

The English teacher Mota Balli actively gave some clueless clues about the active and passive voice sentences to his students, in a low voice although he had the choice of raising his voice.

Later he gave the following sentences to his students and asked them to write the same in the other voice. One student Chota Pilli took advantage of the above instruction and answered the questions below:

Question: Rama killed Ravana

Answer: Rama was not killed by Ravana

Question: Moon is the son of the Sun

Answer: The Sun could be either the father or mother of the moon

Question: Football is the national sport of many Latin American countries Answer: Some Latin American countries don't play football

Question: Both Hollywood and Bollywood produced some most beautiful actresses

Answer: Tollywood Kollywood and livelihood produced the balance of the most beautiful Actresses.

Question: India has become more reputed and popular among most of the nations In the world.

Answer: Narendra Modi visited most of the countries in the world

Question: Google and Twitter have terminated the services of thousands of their employees

Answer: The rest of the MNCs have recruited all these terminated employees, Without terminating their own employees.

Question: Indians are crazy about Cricket, Cinema, and Politics

Answer: Cricket players' cinema heroes and politicians are crazy about money

Question: In India, next to Lord Ram with billions of followers, Adani is the lord of millions of rupees

Answer: Lord Ram is not on the Fortune 500 list but Adani is.

Question: Devotion to Religion does not imply devotion to Spirituality.

Answer: Devotion is the day watchman and Spirituality is the night-watchman

Question: Money is not everything but there is no happiness without some money.

Answer: Some money can give only some happiness but the sum of the money minus some money, if spared, can give happiness to so many.

* * *

Thought
Five-point charter

In a world of opposites, here are my experienced words of life, shared as a five-point charter.

1. Time, place, and environment of birth have a significant impact on one's upbringing, growth, and progress. You're an advanced person if born in the US and not so if born in any other place.
2. Inborn talents are like the crucial junctions in the road map of one's career. We can notice such traits in many scientists, prodigies, and other legends.
3. The people with whom one mingles and moves, could be either a jack to push one up positively or hijack to a den of dungeon of chaos and disorder. One can appreciate this aspect with many people of fame. Our own lives itself could be apt examples as well.
4. The degree of wisdom and maturity of an individual is in no way, less important in moulding one's character and attitude. People over sixty only, generally talk about lessons and learnings of life and are accepted as mature by virtue of their vast experiences.

5. Destiny is the ultimate Managing director in disguise in our every act of daily drama and cinema (Satyajit Ray, Steven Spielberg, Yash Chopra, Manirathnam, Balachandar, like are no way any match for this invisible and invincible Director of our fate). Fortunately or unfortunately this director is irreplaceable in one's lifetime.

Destiny is like a serpent tied to one's leg. Having tried to be over-smart with a minuscule lecture, let me reveal one open secret. Even without any of the above panchasheel (five points) elements, one can live and even thrive in this world, jolly well happily, provided one has the guts and wits, confidence with courage, perseverance with determination, and such associated positive and powerful duos. However, such people are insignificant in number and are ever ready to live even if they have to die.

Humour

Armstrong is enjoying his second wife, I mean, second life on the moon.

Bernard Shaw was the greatest sadist, oh sorry satirist of his time.

Hitler was the coolest, I mean the cruellest man on the earth.

Oscar is given to Americans only sorry to only those liked by Americans.

Osho Rajneesh never owned, sorry, never loaned Mercedes.

London is the lousiest, I mean, loveliest capital of England.

Europe has many capitals, I mean only one capital 'E".

Bill Gates is the founder of Microwave, no, no, Microsoft.

The first founder of Apple was Steve Jobs, oh no, Newton.

Mahatma Gandhi talked more walked less, sorry, the vice versa
Nehru was married and so was Mountbatten, um, um, Lady Mountbatten
Dev Anand did not act in any Hindi movie, I mean French movie.'
Kishore Kumar married only two women at a time, sorry, one woman.

Thought
Keep yourself active

Whether you're occupied or idle, keep your mind and body fit!
Whether others give you a smile or not, smile more with yourself!
Whether someone appreciates it or not, give others your help!
Whether you are cheerful or not, don't lose happiness!
Whether you eat cherry or berry, don't ever worry!
Whether you're married or not, feel always young!
Whether you have close friends or not, befriend yourself!
Whether cheerio, sorrow, or narrow, say no to 'borrow'!
Whether others care about you or not, take the best care of yourself!
Whether it's summer or monsoon, don't forget to laugh every day!
Whether ills or evils, smile and laugh are the pills to kill them!
Whether you're busy or not, keep yourself active!

* * *

Thought
The ninety-five and five per cent

We are living in a world that attaches the utmost significance to money and many materialistic matters. It is natural that an abundant number of people stay tuned to this concept, due to compulsions of circumstances and their choice. Being blessed or cursed with a mind that is like a two-sided coin, we pause now and then to stare at the coin's tail side which tends to give jolts and bumps in our minds. The tail side always tries to caution us about being and behaving like a loving person.

We listen to the sermons of the tail side only to counter the ill effects of the ingrained attitude of living our lives without heeding to conscience. But eventually, the head side, the desire, temptation, greed, and lust for money on the one hand and the instincts of passion and ambition, to attain power and fame, on the other hand, pull us away from the mainstream of divine love.

The result is what we see in this world. You call it deteriorating values, dangerously fast and mechanical routine, and self-centric intentions. A huge chunk of the population, talks, walks, jog and run after the money and its infinite avatars. The balance, the minority, tries to think and act with conscience either due to their nature of adhering to righteous living or for fear of accumulating sins and going to hell.

The two divisions of people i.e. huge chunk and the minority keep swapping from one group to the other, depending upon various factors such that the head of the life coin smiles gleefully at us 95% of the time and its tile side (conscience) pretends to smile 5% of the times.

* * *

Humour
Indian couple in Qatar, watching FIFA matches

Messi Mami: Why India is not playing here?
Peele Sami: The main reason is, most of the time, most of the people, including most of the players, mostly play politics and not football.

Messi Mami: When all the other players are playing only with their feet, why only two players are acting like villains, stopping the balls from going into the net?
Peele Sami: Those two are goalkeepers. They are not supposed to let the football into the net.

Peele Sami: Koreans and Japanese players look similar. But the Argentina and Tunisian players don't look alike, why?
Messi Mami: Good question but the answer is simple. Korea and Japan have five letters each whereas Argentina has nine letters while Tunisia has only seven letters. Obviously, they look different.

Messi Mami: When the Netherlands, Switzerland, Poland, and England have been included in the world cup why Ashok Leyland has been omitted?

Peele Sami: While these countries roll the football, Ashok Leyland rolls out only vehicles. If they start rolling out football, maybe they can claim their stake in the next world cup.
Peele Sami: Now the score is tied up 1-1, extra time is also over. The result will be decided based on the penalty shootout.
Messi Mami: I hate these rules of greed and violence.

Peele Sami: What are you talking about?
Messi Mami: When both the teams have scored one each, they should announce both the teams, victorious. They have not done that. So it is undemocratic.

Peele Sami: I see, ok, what is violence here?
Messi Mami: you say penalty shootout. Is not shootout a terrible violence?
Messi Mami: You say Cameroon's player Abubakar has been given a yellow and red card. Abubakar has not received the card from the referee on both occasions. Maybe that is the reason why he is upset and has left the field abruptly.
Peele Sami: I told you, back in India, to read the basic rule book of international football before coming here to watch world cup football matches. You have not done that.
Messi Mami: I have been watching since the beginning of this match. That man in the black dress keeps running with the players but has never kicked the ball even once. But he is trying to boss over every player by whistling, staring, and scolding them. What does he think of himself?
Peele Sami: Referee

* * *

Thought
Big thanks to every charity

Bill Gates donating huge sums for charity is fine; Elon Musk spending millions for noble causes is ok; Ambani, contributing crores for humanitarian causes is good; Adanis giving away large funds for NGOs is all right; Tatas, contributing magnanimously for the welfare of the poor and the needy is laudable.

At the same time, one could easily make out that all these icon figures and organizations started charity only after penetration into the markets and making big value additions to their capitals and sizable profits. Interestingly, it can be observed that the percentage of net profit donated by such entities stands between one and two, based on the past average. On a higher scale, it could be around six to eight per cent, in the case of enormous profit-making companies, notwithstanding the inconsistency in the charities, so contributed.

For rich people, celebrities, and giant corporates, giving for charity have got twin advantages, i.e. Enhanced publicity and reduced tax liability. The acts of donations are win-win combinations for them. Increased publicity results in increased business, adding to their reputation, name, and brand image. From another angle, sparing funds for social causes is nothing but extended Corporate Social Responsibility (CSR) as stipulated by law. On the other hand, if such corporate houses and individuals don't give for charity, the press and media are out there, watching with a third eye so as to indulge in some skirmishes. So, one can logically deduce the reasoning behind donations made by celebrity people and the top 50 companies in the limelight, both within the country and across the world.

If charity is part of one's character of compassion and attitude of service to the community, such acts are worth admirable for their supreme nature. If an individual or company ends up with a loss due to donating to charity, such individuals and entities deserve to be described as champions for society.

I don't deny the fact that whether given out of compassion or with other motives, charity is a fine as well as noble act worth praising because it goes out to help NGOs or downtrodden people to benefit from such a charity.

It is also to be accepted and appreciated that there are some rich people, celebrities, and organizations who donate silently without any publicity and commercial expectations. Hats off to them!

I sum up as below:

A daily wage earner shelling out a hundred for charity is Adorable

A low-income group man sparing five hundred is Commendable

A middle-class man, donating two thousand rupees is Admirable

An orphan, earning and giving back to the orphanage is Laudable

Acts of charity by rich celebrities and organizations are Verifiable!

Humour

I went to a supermarket. It was 10 PM. They said, "You will get only supper. No other goods". Then I thought "It was just a supper market".

* * * *

I went to a departmental store. I asked, "I want to visit the sales department". They said, "We are selling our products in the Purchase Department. So the purchasing department is the sales department where you can purchase what we sell."

* * * *

I went to a small retail shop. I asked for a pack of biscuits. Rs.20/- was mentioned as its MRP. When I paid Rs.20/- the shopkeeper asked me to pay Rs.25/-. Taken by surprise I asked him "The MRP is Rs.20/-, How can you charge Rs.25/-? He told me, more with a sober voice "My wife is so fond of these biscuits and consumes 10 packs daily. Then, please tell me how to make up for the loss"

* * * *

Thought
Living in the moment

There are plenty of ways to invite problems and worries. But there is absolutely only one way to give a send-off to these problems and worries. Everyone knows what that way is and says many words about it in a day. It is called conscious awareness. This is the double-edged knife. When one becomes more and more aware of himself, his inner thoughts, and the external surroundings and starts acting accordingly, one may feel jittery, anxious, stressed, frightened, guilty, delirious, and undergo all such sorts of experiences. Yes, that is the first sign and step to diving deep into conscious awareness.

To become self-conscious and aware is to be alone in a state of silence and plunge into one's inner self. In the process, the tastes and wastes of the past come gushing heavily and engulf one's mind. Depending on the nature of the happenings and incidents the aroma of guilt, fear, disgust, and hatred, attacks the seeker, lightly or heavily. Such a state of mind may persist even for a long time. But the seeker should not give up observing himself with all awareness. The sub-conscious mind keeps one, away from conscious thinking due to habits cultivated for decades.

Every time when the negative past tries to attack the seeker, he should not give up but brush aside that nagging past. The more one lingers in the past, the more the remains of its waste. When one keeps diving deep into oneself with more and more awareness, one would appreciate that the moment present is the best time to live happily. Neither the past nor the future can give the immense joy the present moment gives.

As so beautifully articulated by JK (J. Krishnamurthy) a person should die every moment to live in the present which is nothing but getting rid of the past, even things that happened an hour earlier. This practice does not guarantee a person instant salvation, freedom, or a magical solution to his problems. Everything that has to happen will happen as destined but the person becomes more balanced and equanimous so that he doesn't get upset or jolted by things of the past.

Yes, the past never stops peeping in now and then but is shown the exit in no time. In the process, one can hang on more and more to the present state of joy and can live a far better life with courage and confidence. Of course, it is left to the individual as to how he carves out the present. When courage and confidence become like the two hands of a person, nothing can stop his smile, cheers, laughter, and superior quality of joy, except the person himself.

* * *

Humour

A speeding ambulance on an emergency call bypassed almost every red signal on its way to the caller's house. The same ambulance once again sped to the hospital, bypassing every red signal, carrying the ambulance's driver in its rear seat with the oxygen mask on him. The patient who was supposed to be brought in the ambulance drove the ambulance to the hospital. The ambulance driver was admitted to the ICU with chest pain while the alleged patient was treated in the OP for waist pain.

It turned out that the patient who was to be brought in the ambulance was the wife of the ambulance's driver, who knew driving. She slipped into the bathroom, cracking its floor but she herself had no pain. Still, she wanted to ensure everything was all right with her and called the emergency number for ambulance assistance. The driver of the ambulance happened to be her ex-husband who divorced her for ill-treating him.

It appears that his ex-wife demanded he lay in the rear seat with the oxygen mask while she drove the ambulance.

To their disbelief, the hospital authorities found their ambulance driver along with the ambulance missing. It was later ascertained that the ambulance driver's wife joined as a nurse in the same hospital and posted in the ICU where her ex-husband was being treated. It seems she did not allow him to eat any food but administered him only medicines in overdose. The hospital hired a new ambulance and a driver. After a week's time, the new ambulance driver was admitted to the ICU for fear phobia. One doctor, who wanted to be anonymous, told a patient in the OP that the new ambulance driver borrowed Rs.5000/- from the nurse, the ex-wife of the ex-ambulance driver but could not repay. On seeing him in the hospital, the nurse landed ten punches on his face and extremely twisted his hands. She was fined Rs.20000 by the hospital authorities for doing this, which she paid promptly. The hospital gave Rs.10000 to the new ambulance driver towards compensation and he in turn, gave the same to the nurse saying that Rs.5000 he borrowed ten years ago must have become Rs.10000 now and also he had only that much amount to repay his loan along with interest. While the new ambulance driver was being discharged after the medical treatment, the nurse seemed to have warned him "You better get me the remaining amount of Rs.10000 within two months or else I will break your already broken face and twist your head in such a way that you could see only the things happening behind you". Some reliable sources in the hospital said that he had already applied for a PF loan of Rs.10000/-. Still interesting is the news that the original ambulance driver was the elder brother of the new ambulance driver. The new ambulance driver was also a divorcee for being a teetotaler.

Thought
Seventy-five years of Independence

The green revolution made agriculture lucrative with export
The White Revolution solved milk availability to every family
Nuclear tests have warned the world "India is a superpower
Polio eradication has put us on the health map of the world
Putting the spacecraft into Mar's orbit put India's head high
Isn't two hundred Crs jabs post-covid-19, a laudable work?
Isn't 100 unicorn startups in three years a noteworthy feat?
How about raising the bar of life expectancy from 32 to 70?
Where was the 14% literacy rate, where it is now at 78%?
Nobel, Olympics, and Oscar now embrace us now, isn't it?
The spiritual capital of the world has always been India
Non-violence is India's precious gift for the human race
Our rich cultural heritages are indeed, a global treasure
India is ruled by democracy and democracy rules India!
The rich cap worn by every Indian has certain black spots
Women folks are still kept far away from the public spaces
India's gender equality gap in the world, is 114, a big zero
The habit of seeing women as the soft-preys, persists still
There is a deep dent and downfall in our rich value system
Enough, clamouring 'Proud India' and 'Proud Indians' glamour
It is time to introspect ourselves so that we get more respect
We should have put on a far better show in the past 75 years

From now whenever we hoist the tricolour, we must feel proud
Not for the heck of it but for transforming our country as great!

Thought
God from different eyes

God is an idea as per Einstein
God is a concept as per philosophers
God is a catalyst as per God-thinkers
God is a watch-dog as per hell believers
God is the supreme king as per many subjects
God is the universe's caretaker as per God-worshippers
God is abstract as per rational reformists
God is omnipresent as per Hindu philosophy
God is all as per universal moral belief
God is nothing (nothingness) as per cult groups
There is no God; this is the conviction of non-believers

God is pristine love, eternal peace, and divine happiness
Provided one could feel, experience, and realize deep inside!
This is the opinion of Joyram!

Humour

1. Abdul forgets things very easily. He lived in Kabul for a long time.

2. Babul normally gets good grades in his academics. He was born in Belgrade.
3. Cutebull sings classical raag 'Kanada' so well. The reason is he lives in Canada.
4. Dorothy is a good dubbing artist. She was educated in Dublin.
5. Eversleep remained ever slow forever in his life after climbing Everest.
6. Frankenstein was always frank in his talks. Thanks to his hometown Frankfurt.
7. Glasgow has to wear reading glasses always. He lives in Glasgow.
8. Hanna swallowed so much hamburger while she stayed in Hamburg.
9. Indu went to a Mall and felt it was like a continent, she is a resident of Mal (Asia).
10. Jambu lives with his wife Jammu in a jungle house located in Jammu

* * *

Thought
A dignified message

This is a testified world of mystified uncertainty that is verified by billions of people and certified by every horrified human who has been qualified to clarify. Even dignified people are terrified with awe by the never-ending good, bad, bitter, and worst in every individual and society. Even a thoroughly satisfied person cannot remain so for a long time due to the unpredictable nature of time. One must become dissatisfied after being satisfied. It is clarified by even many bonafide people, that people of divine character are always crucified at the end, however, fortified they may remain. Hence, the life lesson is one should live ever, modified.

* * *

Humour

Toothless Dental Clinic
Doctor: What is the problem?
Patient: Toothache
Doctor: which tooth?
Patient: Bluetooth
Doctor: Run away before I remove your entire white teeth.

* * *

Patient: I lost two teeth during a fight with my wife.
Doctor: How could she dismantle two teeth in one go?
Patient: Both were artificial teeth. During one such natural fight, all of a sudden she asked me to open my mouth. As usual, when I obeyed, she pulled out the two artificial teeth in no time and threw them out of the window from the fifteenth floor of our apartments.
Doctor: Ok. Don't get dentally upset. I will replace them with ceramic-coated strong teeth.

Patient: What is the guarantee that my wife will not remove the new teeth as well?
Doctor: Just don't open your mouth in front of her.
Patient???
Doctor: You are laughing at everything I say, what should I infer?
Patient: You are a good joker.
Theatre assistant: I wonder why you waited for more than six months with such excruciating pain without removing the decayed teeth earlier.
Patient: My wife is deeply interested in my anatomy and she is also a savings buff. Six months ago when I complained that I have a decayed tooth, she opened my mouth and told me that two teeth had already decayed and another two were likely to get decayed in the next few months. She suggested I don't remove the decayed tooth, immediately but get the four decayed teeth extracted together so that we could save on 1. Cost of anaesthesia 2. Cost of extraction and 3. Post-extraction medicines and 4. Possible quantity discount.
The theatre assistant was shocked and stared at the patient for five long minutes, simultaneously verifying whether he himself (The theatre assistant) had any tooth decay inside his mouth.

* * *

Doctor: What happened to the two ceramic teeth that I fixed on you just fifteen minutes ago?
Patient: your nurse dismantled it.

Doctor: How dare she could?
Patient: When she gave me my medicines I smiled at her and told jokingly "I would like to bite you with my newly fixed ceramic teeth". I never imagined that she would react like a cruel and efficient expert dentist that too merely with her bare hands.

* * *

Thought
I am life for two souls

There are millions of people who don't know me
There are tens and thousands who know me not
There are a few thousand who can recognize me
There are a few hundred who could appreciate me
There are tens of people who might admire me too
There are a handful of people who like and trust me
But there are only two pure souls for whom I am life!

Thought
Make and deploy

Make your legs and hands like active majestic soldiers
Make your eyes and ears as your air force's colonels
Make your lungs and stomach as the Navy's captains
Make your mind as the Supreme commander in chief
Let daily physical exercise be the central- coordinator

Let wise thinking and awareness be your twin-guides
Let silence and meditation be the intellectual advisers
Let a smile and a positive attitude be the full-time security
Deploy confidence and courage in every warfare of life
Deploy determination and willpower in every checkpost
Deploy love and compassion as your military's caterers
Deploy humour and service as your second in command
Now you're empowered to take on any enemy and win!

Humour

A candid interview with me by a BBC correspondent
BBC Correspondent: why have you been born?
Me: What is the other way to celebrate my birthday every year?
BBC: Why have you grown?
Me: If you don't grow up, who would call you a grown-up boy?
BBC: Why did you study?
Me: If I don't do that who would pay the fees to schools and colleges
BBC: why have you chosen employment?
Me: Is that not the only escape to avoid people mocking me as jobless
BBC: Why did you earn?
Me: If one cannot earn a good name then what is left?
BBC: Why did you indulge in love?
Me: Love failure is not possible without loving someone, you must know.
BBC: Why did you get married?
Me: If my wife was to get married, can you suggest any other way, other than marrying her?

BBC: Why did you become a father?

Me: Else, I would have never gotten any promotion in my life

BBC: Then, why did you become a father again?

Me: Everyone knows that promotion comes with more responsibility

BBC: Why did you get angry often?

Me: If I have to limit the number of people I love, this is the only option left.

BBC: Why are you simply vegetating without knowing the survival art?

Me: Can anyone in this world survive with morals, ethics, honesty, commitment, etc? Please tell me honestly.

BBC: Why do you keep writing more than often?

Me: When I had the pen, I did not know what to write. Now, when there is no need for a pen, my idiotic brain keeps thinking, I don't know how to dispense with writing, without a pen.

BBC: Why only twenty copies of each of your two English books, written in the last couple of years, have been sold to date?

Me: There are forty people in this world who think like me. Is this not great joyful news?

BBC: Even after crossing sixty years, why are you so excited to do something?

Me: During my twenties, I did not do what I was supposed to do, nor the opportunities fell for me. Now having learned some life lessons I am eager to share what I have experienced and understood and hence this exit-less excitement of endless experiments.

BBC: Do you have any secrets in your life?

Me: Why should I hesitate to share with you my secrets? But people clamour not to share one's secrets in public. So, when I get an opportunity to meet you in person I will certainly share some of the many secrets of my life if you agree to execute a guarantee bond (on a twenty rupees stamp paper) that you will not disclose to anyone, whatever I told you.

BBC: Why do you claim your life is an open book?

Me: Right since my school days, I never used to close the book after reading. The discipline continues.

The BBC correspondent immediately leaves the house in silence.

Thought
Mostly we copycat

Knowledge is one thing, wisdom is one thing. Not every knowledgeable person has acknowledgeable wisdom and vice versa. Knowledge is gained with an intellectual mind; wisdom is ingrained more by experience. Apart from these, there is something called originality. The sizable population lacks originality. As long as one shapes his mind, dress, attitude, his mannerism, his way of talking, etc in line with what is taught to him, or what one reads and hears, he is nothing but a copycat. Knowingly or unknowingly most of us are copycats in one or the other aspect. Social mannerism is a classic example of copycatting. Sleeping is one thing that people generally can't copycat. It has to be original to have the real benefits of sleeping. People attend courses to learn to speak, write, anchor, act, singing whatnot. Quite a number of them make name and money with such learned skills. But they all copycat basically.

I myself, a small-time singer, till a year ago, copycatted. One reason was I sang mostly the filmy numbers. Be it Mohd. Rafi, Kishore Kumar, Mukesh, Manna De, HemanthKapoorr or Hemanth Kuma, or even Kumar Sanu, I tried to replicate their style of singing. Likewise in Tamil, I used to sing many songs sung by Late T.M.Soundararajan, Late SP Balasubhramanyam, Late P.B.Srinivas, and K.J Yesudas, etc. Believe it or not, for at least a couple of Tamil songs, which I rendered in online apps like Smule and Starmaker, I got feedback that my voice resembled the original singer's voice. But in the case of Hindi songs, I never received such feedback. The reason could be, as far as Tamil songs are concerned, I listened to them since I was three years old and always wanted to sing them as sung by the original playback singer for decades.

Humour

A person after graduation wants employment and after 25 years of employment becomes the employer's monument!

After employment (he) wants to romance and get married, and after a couple of years into the marriage, finds life more of a nuisance and becomes worried!

After the marriage s (he) wants to become a parent, but later comes to appreciate that (he) after all created one patent!

After becoming a parent, s (he) wants to be contented with a family of triangles but soon is lured by the angel of inescapable routine, and makes it as a family of squares!

After becoming a parent of two, s (he) understands that life is nothing but whimsical, physical, statistical, vocal, and more than these, hysterical and mechanical.

And that's the point of the great realization in life that s (he) should have pursued BE (Supplied and Applied Psychology) at the University of Babilonia instead of being bogged down by BE (Replied and Implied Mechanical) at the University of 'Coronalia'

* * *

Thought
The reality

A young man, with a passion and voice for singing, sitting on an easy chair at his home, eyeing to become an ordinary singer in the future, who is also desirous of making a couple of best friends in life, envisioning his life's last days, as sitting on the same chair, was not the reality.

He has now grown into a sixty-plus figure. Destiny made him survive ordinarily but not with an ordinary attitude. Time bestowed on him an education that liked him but that education was not liked by him, thrusting on him a career that was never cherished by him or relished by his employer. That was the reality.

In the prime of his youth, he was removed from his native place. The only two friends, with whom he moved without inhibitions, whom he hoped would be his best, eventually turned out as worst in the time burst. That was the reality.

He is presently confined, merely as a singer of his life's voice, not as listeners' choice. Of late, he made entry into writing, his goods of writings, with the flavours of puns, cut bits of wits, punches in inches, and philosophical sprinklings are mostly hidden in the open rail yard that has no rail track. That is the reality.

The unfortunate fortune keeps smiling at his cascading eyes (which he feels could be a phenomenon of joyful tears), trying to console him but in fact depriving him of any marked progress and delight, in the twilight of his life. This is the beauty of the ugly reality of cruelty served in plenty, in his empty life plate of complete uncertainty. That is the reality.

Humour

A lioness stayed within the cave till the lion came back to the cave because the lion drew a line at the entrance of the cave and told the lioness “Cheetah, sorry, Sita, don’t cross this line, otherwise you may end up crossing the railway line”.

1. In a quiz session conducted by the education minister Fox in the Palace of the Lion, only one rabbit won the rapid round questions.
2. The male bear told the female “I told you many times not to drink too much beer. Now you see, you are not able to bear your own weight”.
3. The tigers in the woods waited eagerly to catch the ball from the other side, hit by the classic golf player Tiger Woods.
4. The Tamil elephant laughed uncontrollably when he saw his little rat (Eli in Tamil) friend, wearing a pant, and shouted with excitement “Eli pants” ‘Eli pants”.

Back in Chennai, two friendly dogs meet after a long time. One dog tells the other “Nowadays, my barking doesn’t invite anyone's attention because my Master shouts much louder and longer than me". The other dog said, "Oh, it is surprising. In my house, my Master remains always calm but only his wife yells at him even for nothing. If I ever bark at some stray dogs including strange humans, she yells at me and the stray dogs and strange humans vanish in no time".

* * *

Thought
About teachers and their contributions

Which is the noble profession in today's world?

Unquestionably it is the teacher's profession!

Who is a teacher?

Any person from whom someone learns something

What is their role?

To make the other know, appreciate; learn certain subject matter that would in turn enrich the learner's knowledge.

Are teachers not confined to the teaching staff at schools and other educational institutions?

No. Along with every newborn child, two teachers are also born invariably.

Teachers in the school play a vital role in shaping the aptitude and attitude and even the character of a student and that's why their role as teachers gains more significance.

Rest in every other field, where one gets unadulterated knowledge on anything, on any subject or field of specialization, even in the realms of social, ethical, and moral behaviour, the one who clarifies, trains, explains and teaches gets into the shoes of a teacher. The other person by default becomes the student.

Why teacher's role is so important?

A teacher, by virtue of their position, is in a position to influence the other person, to a certain extent, in the subject matter taught. The other person by default or conviction registers whatever is taught, according to one's grasping ability. This goes a long way in shaping their knowledge, behaviour, and to some extent attitude as well, which will serve as the root in shaping one's career and way of living, along with the incidental academic performance.

Is teaching and preaching one and the same?

Preaching can be a part of teaching but not the other way.

While teaching enables one to acquire knowledge and reap wisdom, Preaching tries to condition the mind for religious and moral adherence.

Why Teachers' day is celebrated on 5th September of every year?

That day is the birthday of the Late President Dr Sarvapalli Radhakrishnan, the great teacher, thinker, and philosopher. In order to honour his noble services in the teaching profession, this day is celebrated as 'Teachers'Dayy'. Incidentally, this day also marks the death anniversary of Late Mother Teresa, the Nobel laureate. So to say, today is the convergence of Noble and Nobel champions.

Humour

1. Friend 1: what did you pray at the temple?

Friend 2: For my remarriage

Friend 1: what happened to your first wife?
Friend 2: She is already remarried

* * *

2. Friend 1: What is the secret of your 50 years of married life?
Friend 2: Daily we sleep in two bedrooms
Friend 1: Great, so you sleep together in two bedrooms every day.
Friend 2: No, we sleep separately in two bedrooms. Yes, we do swap the bedrooms sometimes.
Friend 1: Hope you are having wonderful times after marriage.
Friend 2: Your statement is like asking a blind person 'Are you enjoying the beauty of nature'?

* * *

Friend 1: Who is that lady who has been dancing with those six men?
Friend 2: She is celebrating her sixth successful divorce with her ex-husband.

* * *

Friend 1: What do you do for your livelihood, now that you don't have any employment?
Friend 2: I give counselling to people in my neighbourhood. I give certain secret tips for becoming an artist in Bollywood, Kollywood and Bollywood movies.

Thought
A big festival with small rituals

Lord Ganesh's head was truncated by Lord Shiva. It symbolizes the removal of ego from our minds. His head was replaced with an elephant's head. This symbolized the due honour given even to an animal. With the head of an elephant, Ganesh looks majestic, without head weight we can be more realistic.

Ganapathy's cute stomach is portrayed as large and massive. This is compatible with his elephant's head. The matching concept symbolizes the need for synchronization of one's thoughts and actions in honing one's character. Lord Lambodara sitting on a mouse appears inconsistent and absurd even. But the message to be inferred is 'even amidst the numerous worldly problems, one can feel light and happy, and that is how life is to be lived.

The massive ears of the Lord Gajamukh indicate 'one can become wise by listening more than speaking and blabbering one-sided'. God Vinayaka is shown holding 'mothakam' (sweet made of rice flour and jaggery) in his hands without eating it, which can be interpreted that those, having surplus wealth, can always hold and spend a portion of it for noble causes.

The four hands of God send a clear message that Courage, self-determination, faithfulness, and divinity should always be one's armour to ward off any obstacles in life.

The attractive attire is to appreciate the fact that living is both for enjoyment and service To mankind. Life on earth is really worth it only when indulged in genuine pleasures, Cautiously and consciously, commensurate with one's wealth.

Finally, the multiple names attributed to the Lord show that the ultimate super God is one, irrespective of the number of religions and other divisions. Let us not believe or register in our minds that Lord Shiva truncated Ganesha's head. Such an act would be the last thing any Godhead would indulge in. As expressed above, these are stories of symbolic nature with valuable messages for the welfare and well-being of the human race.

Past is tense because it is devoid of any taste and is a waste in the present
The present tense is the boon to relish the feast of the present that is present
Future will be the toast of the cake, roasted or burnt, as it's baked at present

Thought
Something to Nothing

What we learn as students is something; what we achieve as the learned is nothing
What we indulge as a youth is something; what we deliver is nothing
What we strive for in our career is something; what we accomplish is nothing
What we want in life is something; what we derive is nothing
What we aim to become is something; what we become is nothing
We keep working in life for something, and finally, we end up with 'nothing'
Nothing is better than nonsense; hence being nothing makes some sense.

Humour
Holi hangover

If you can afford to have a car of your own, then you truly become a sarkar!

* * *

If Moody ranks India as still a developing country, don't get upset there's Modi!

* * *

'Hot' has T, Biscuit has T, pastry has T, how can there be a party without Tea?

* * *

As long as Putin remains stubborn, peace between Russia and Ukraine is Katin

* * *

If you want to live with Kangaroos go to Australia, if you want to live with Pandas be in China
If you want to live with snow dogs go to Antarctica, if you want to live with capital settle down in the US and if you want to live with dignity don't leave India!

* * *

However, one who is open, honest, and transparent is compelled to undergo a change in their colours on Holi (day)!

* * *

Thought
Smiling at every stage of life

A baby smiles at everyone it is a manifestation of innocence
A fifteen-year grownup smiles discreetly out of adolescence
A youth smiles at their peers driven more by a romantic sense
A middle-aged person smiles safeguarding against nuisance
Older ones think before smiling due to caution in abundance
A jolly person smiles uninhibited realizing what life's essence

Humour
Fuss in the Bus

Conductor: Where would you like to get down?
Passenger: In the next stop after three stops
Conductor: Where did you board the bus?
Passenger: Two stops before the last three stops.
(Conductor stops the bus before the stop ahead and asks the passenger to get down)

* * *

Passenger: Yesterday I missed this bus
Conductor: How did you miss it?
Passenger: I missed going to the office.
Conductor: Why? What happened? Whether someone at home is not well?
Passenger: No. It was a holiday for my office.

* * *

Conductor to the newly joined driver: When I give one whistle you should stop the bus.
Driver: OK
Conductor: When I give two whistles you can move the bus from the bus stop.
After the bus started from the terminus, the conductor gives a whistle at the next stop. But the driver didn't stop the bus.
The conductor goes to the driver and tells him "Stop the bus, I told you to stop when I give one whistle".
After the passengers boarded, the conductor gives two whistles. The driver did not move the bus. The conductor got a bit irritated and said "What happened? I told you should keep the bus moving when I give two whistles."
The amused driver replied: I waited for you to give me one whistle before I stopped the bus, but you didn't give me one. Now, I am waiting for you to give me two whistles to move the bus. So three whistles are already pending from you.

* * *

Thought
The majority and the minority

As far as the overwhelming majority, life is an opportunity to live as one likes!
Out of the overwhelming majority, the majority think life is for material and sensual pleasures!
As far the majority in the majority of the overwhelming majority, life is a gift of God for living and enjoying but with certain discipline!

As for the rest of the majority, life is just random luck and happens on its own, without any superpower controlling it! (Atheists)
As for those in the minority, life is given by God and is to be lived by thinking and thanking every day, with an eye to getting birth in heaven!
As far the as minority within the minority, life is due to one's past deeds, one has to keep taking birth after birth, until the soul reaches a perfect 'no-desire' stage when the soul merges with the supreme soul, with no more birth and death. If anyone doesn't fit in any of the above principles, they must be sent to some unseen and unknown universe, not known to our universe!

Thought
What are A, B, C, D, and E?

Let anything happen inside your mind!
Let crisis and adversity strike your mind!
Watch them, stare at them, and witness them without reacting or interacting!
As you keep observing them, they move or fade away on their own!
Be bold and courageous, when problems invade you or you invite them of your own!
You don't have to remember all the 26 alphabets always, but you must remember the first five of them, every day, every moment...
Just remember A, B, C, D, and E expanded as" Always Be Courageous, Determined and Enthusiastic"

If you could practice this simple suggestion, you will enjoy more and more unadulterated happy times!

Some childhood fries from my hot thought pan!

When I was a child, I tasted drops of kerosene and that was the first time I was administered

Medicine!

Even as a boy I used to Christine's names on others, one such name given to a girl who walked, self-circling, was 'top on the ground'!

I felt my first pinch at age six, when my elder brother pinched my upper arm, sharply whenever I

Spoke any word, while going to school in his company!

I was afraid (even now) of ghosts but never felt so when I, Master Black 13, wore a ghostly black dress and black glasses, in the pitch dark, knocked on the door and terrified my woman-tenant, during a power cut in the night, almost killing her!

Feeling jealous of my naming fame, one of my schoolmates made me more popular by awarding me the Nickname, 'Buffalo's Milkman'!

Thought
A small questionnaire

Who am I?

Ponder over this question as often.

Why am I here?

Think over this question now and then.

What is my role?

Enquire about this aspect in totality.
What is the purpose of life?
Rewind, pause, forward, and conclude.
Am I satisfied with my life?
Probe this deeply and opine yourself.
What gives me real peace and happiness?
Search, research, and reach the answer.
What is the most important thing I want at this stage of my life?
Choose from the various available choices.
How can I derive more peace and joy?
List out the possible alternatives, and pick the befitting.
Do I wish to receive more or give more?
Be truthful and come out with a clear response.
How much more do I want to live, given my health and wealth conditions?
Analyze the past, look into the present, try to foresee the future, and express in years. Answer to your best.
After answering this questionnaire sincerely with an open mind, you would find yourself at least, a shade different in all respects.

Humour

The graceful motivational speaker sister B.K. Shivani; The world's best wicket-keeper captain M.S.Dhoni; The first cricketer who acted as a Hero, Saleem Durrani; The firebrand politician turned octogenarian L.K. Advani; The leg spinner who cast a magic spell in his debut Narendra Hirwani; The evergreen Indian business tycoon Reliance's Mukesh Ambani;

Every sherwani-wearing and parishani-bearing Sahani, Motwani, Kidwani, Badlani, and Mathani including every abhimani; every devoted listener of AIR, the Akashvani;
All were perplexed, confounded, and silently threatened with anxiety and grave concern about the abrupt withdrawal of the 20K Crores Follow-on Public offer by the Indian business magnate Gautam Adani.

* * *

Thought
Gandhi Jayanthi

Non-violence was the artillery Gandhiji deployed
While simplicity was the weapon Sastryji carried
Lal Bahadur was non-violence's true ambassador
Mahatma was simplicity's champion and crusader
Sastryji's death in Russia was shrouded in mystery
Mahatma's assassination by Godse is now history
The role model of honesty was the late Mr Kamaraj
Only during his rule did Tamil Nadu see the Ramraj
Even after learning from these great noble leaders
Are we following their virtues beyond the corridors?
Don't we see violence of all sorts across the country?
Are we not mesmerized easily by the Western world?
Is there even a single government without corruption?
To arrest violence we need more Gandhis in our country
Not just those with family and nicknames such as Gandhi
To make honesty a way of life, people must make the way
Observing vigilance and vigil in daily life could be the way

Development is inevitable and progress is unavoidable
But any amount of prosperity is useless and despicable
If our time-tested morals and ethics are made negotiable
Let us first unite and take an oath to make India enviable!

Thought
Living in the present

Whenever one is upset with the past, he tends to set up a dark future. But, instead, if a person brushes aside the past, however awesome and gruesome it may be, and stop worrying about the future scenario, however rosy or sorrowful it may appear to be, he would enjoy painting a beautiful drawing of the present. Such a drawing will enthuse and improvise one to remain in the present steadfast.

Humour

A saint, unmistakenly guided by a mistaken GPS ends up in a politician's house. The following conversation ensues:
Saint: Hope I am in the right place in the house of Mr Silky Srikanth
Politician: I am Milky Srikant, owner of the milk sweet brand "Srikant of Thashkant'
Saint: Silky or milky that is not a big issue. It would be catchier if your brand is called "Srikant of Nilkant". You visited my ashram last year and met me personally. Didn't you?
Politician: I have met many saints in my life but I don't remember to have seen you. Where is your ashram?

Saint: I have ashrams in Annanagar, Bangalore, Coimbatore, Dindigul, Erode, Faridabad, Gandhinagar, Himalayas, Indore, Jugu Beach, Kolkatta, Ludhiana, Mangalore, Nagaland, Orissa, Panipat, Quilon, Rajkot, Secunderabad, Thailand, Uruguay, Vienna, Washington, Xiangpeng, Yeman, and Zimbabwe.

Politician (almost faining): I too have bank accounts in many branches but only in two countries, India and Switzerland. How could you establish ashrams in AtoZ places?

Saint: I just established my connection not with any railway guard or night guard but with the real God. The Almighty helped me establish my ashrams in these places. I am planning, oh, sorry, God is planning to establish another 26 ashrams for me.

Politician: I can't even imagine where you are going to put up these ashrams but I am damn sure that these ashrams will be built in places starting from alphabet A to Z.

Saint: I am surprised that you have some common sense too.

Politician: Without that, no one can survive in this world, not even, the so-called saints.

Saint: I know what you people do to make extra money. Surely, they are not earned through the right means.

Politician: Yes, it is not through right means but 'left means, right?' By the way who gives you money for building A to Z number of ashrams?

Saint: Mostly politicians like you. They give donations of lakhs of rupees. For having already spent ten precious minutes of mine with you, you must be feeling to contribute at least a few lakhs for building my upcoming ashrams. Right now one is coming up in Antarctica. Your donation will directly get frozen there. Contribute before you turn cold.

Politician: Right now I am not in the ruling party. Maybe if our party wins the next general elections, I might think of contributing to your Zambia ashram.

Saint: I wonder how you could make it so correct about my plans to establish an ashram in Zambia.

Politician: Even a schoolboy would say that. What follows after Zimbabwe is Zambia.

By the way, May I know your name, Saint Ji?

Saint: EPF

Politician: What is EPF, Employees Provident Fund?

Saint: Empty Purse Fellow

Politician: What is the need for you to have a purse, you say you are a saint.

Saint: Earlier many of my disciples used to say humbly "Swami Ji, your name is EPF but you don't carry any purse at all. It will be more appropriate if you carry a purse without money in it." Since then I started to keep a purse that contains not even a single penny but only credit cards.

Politician: Why only credit cards, you can keep debit cards as well.

Saint: That would reflect my creditworthiness negatively.

Politician: For a saint having his name as 'Fellow' doesn't give dignity. Why don't you change the fellow into Fakhir and call yourself an 'Empty Purse Fakhir'?

Saint: Your suggestion is good but then let me tell you how I ended up as a 'Fellow'. Once I applied for 'Fellow of the Royal Society', London. After considering my credentials, they told me "At the most, we can give you the title of 'Fellow' without the suffix 'of Royal Society'.

At that, I jokingly said "Instead of' 'Fellow' I would prefer 'the title 'God's buffalo'.

The committee members got a little wild with my above suggestion. One of their committee members said in a sarcastic tone "We initially thought of giving you the title 'Mr. Follow' because many so-called disciples follow you and you don't follow anybody. But when someone addresses you as "Mr Follow', you may start following them, wherever they go. So, be contended with the title "Mr Fellow".

Politician: Enough of cock and bull stories, I mean, fellow, and buffalo stories.

(Saying these, the politician, who has already pulled off three of the buttons from his shirt, without knowing he was doing that, suddenly tears open his shirt as well and starts running on the road, barefoot)

Thought
We arrive only to depart

Every day arrives certainly but only to depart
Every association is entered only to part with
Every relationship is tied up only to stay apart
Every friendship is forged only to die naturally
Every pleasure comes only to sicken one later
Every moment takes us only towards final-end
Every WhatsApp Msg is not stored but deleted!

Humour

A train passenger to the Enquiry assistant at the Railway station:

Passenger: Is Rajdhani express is running late by one hour?

Assistant: Sorry, we can confirm that only after 2 hours…...

At the bus station:

Passenger to the Enquiry Assistant: Where is the conductor of this bus?

Assistant: In the driver's seat………

At the pilgrimages centre:

Pilgrim to the Enquiry assistant: When the temple will open?

Assistant: When the watchman opens it……………

At the Cinema Theatre where only 50% seating is permitted:

Movie buff: Is there any special offer for buying this movie ticket?

Counter clerk: Yes. Pay for one seat and get one seat free……

Outside a Circus show:

Circus fan: Do you have the 'Lady on the Lion' show today?

Counter clerk: NO.Y/day the lady was a bit late to sit on the lion. The lion became furious and sat on the lady. The lady is now at 'Lion's Fees Hospital for realignment of her body to its original shape.

At, another circus show:

A visitor to the counter clerk: Can we get to watch the lady sitting on the lion's item in today's show?

Clerk: Sorry, due to the prevailing pandemic, no admission inside. But she will sit on the lion, online.

In a vegetable shop

Buyer: Why there is no lady's finger today?

Vendor: The lady who went to buy lady's fingers got her fingers cut.

In a sweet shop:

Customer: What is the best sweet, made today?

Vendor: Bitter-taste-snake-gourd halwa

In a hotel:

Customer: Can I have a menu card?

Supplier: Sorry Sir, that is not for consumption

Inside a flight:

Passenger: Why there is so much shaking inside the plane?

Air hostess: The pilot is shaking hands with the co-pilot who is celebrating her birthday today.

Thought
What else is in store?

We waited for a period of innocence;
In a sense, we had it during childhood
We waited for our youth empowerment;
We had it in college by way of romance
We looked up to exhibiting our calibre;
We displayed it in our professional works
We desired to enjoy on a regular basis;
We achieved it through merrymaking marriage
We craved sensual pleasures of many kinds;
We had them but felt discontented afterwards
We did not want problems or burdens in life;
But in fact, we live with them around the clock
What else is in store to enjoy or suffer now?

Humour
The doctor who went into a Coma

Part 1

A patient goes to a hospital. At the receptions counter:

Patient: I have a problem; I want to consult the doctor

Help desk: Sure, please pay Rs.1000/- towards consultation fees

Patient: I have a problem, I don't have Rs.1000/

Help desk: No problem Sir, you can pay by any means, cash, credit or debit card or phone pay

Patient: I have Rs.500/- in cash. I shall pay it now. After consultation, I will pay the balance thru phone pay

Help desk: Sir, you have to pay the entire amount if you want to meet the doctor.

Patient: If I share only 50% of my problems with the doctor now, then Rs.500/- should be no problem!

Help desk: No Sir, no instalments business. You may share 50% of your problems today and the balance tomorrow free of cost.

Visitor: If money is so much of a problem for you, then no problem, I will pay now (He then pays the amount)

Help desk: Thank you for solving my problem sir. Just wait in the lounge. You are problem no: 2, sorry patient no: 2. the 1st patient is with the doctor. Next, it will be your problems. You may wait in the lounge.

Visitor: No problem Madam.

After half an hour the 1st patient comes out of the doctor's room.

Helpdesk addressing Problem no 1: Sir, hope you had no problem expressing your health problems and getting problem-free medical consultation!
Problem no 1: Of course, I did not have any problem explaining my problems. The only problem was the lack of time. The doctor told me he was facing a lot of problems with many of his patients. At least he is glad that I have told all my problems in one go without posing many problems for the doctor.
Helpdesk: Oh, that is fine Sir. Now my problem is to keep the other problematic patients waiting for a long time. Anyway, that is part and parcel of my problem.
Then she informs problem no: 2 "Sir, you may go inside"

* * *

Visitor: Good evening doctor, how are you?
Doctor: I am fine. How about you?
Visitor: I am also fine.
Doctor: Then why are you consulting me?
Visitor: I have some problems
Doctor: Tell me your problems
Patient: I can't tell those problems
Doctor: I am the doctor. You can always share your problems so that I can try to help you
Patient: I have one major problem
Doctor: What is that?
Patient: I can't share my problems with others and that is the problem.
Doctor: No problem. But I am your doctor now. So go ahead, tell your problems
Patient: I can't tell because that is my problem. I can't tell you my problems.

Doctor: Ok. Then what else do you want to tell me?

Patient: I will share something that is not a problem for me

Doctor: Anyway you have paid the consultation fees; tell me what your non-problematic problems are.

Patient: I always smile at other women but not my wife

Doctor: Oh, it is not a major problem; even I myself do the same. But then it is a delicate problem, you know?

Patient: It is not my problem doctor. It is my wife's

Doctor: Oh got it! Tell me about other non-problematic problems.

Patient: I don't smile at my neighbours

Doctor: It is ok. There is no hard and fast rule you should smile at your neighbours.

Patient: But I smile at my female neighbours and the male neighbours complain it is a big problem.

Doctor: oh, but that is already implied in your earlier non-problem

Patient: But my neighbours smile at my wife

Doctor: So what, you smile at their wives and they smile at your wife. What is your problem here?

Patient: No doctor, there is no problem

Doctor: Fine, now share anything else if you want to

Patient: I eat only five times a day. My wife scolds me often for that.

Doctor: That is too bad

Patient: Yes doctor, you got it but my wife doesn't appreciate that.

Doctor: I am with your wife

Patient: But she is at home doctor

Doctor: I meant that I agree with your wife's scolding you.

Patient: It means you are not prepared to solve my problems

Doctor: I can't solve all your problems. Right now I don't know what a problem is and what is not.

Patient: Doctor, please prescribe some good medicine to come out of my problems

Doctor: Without diagnosing properly how can I prescribe medicines?

Patient: Not for me, for my wife

Doctor: Then I need to see her

Patient: But you need to have an appointment to see her

Doctor: Hey, it is the other way around. I neither want to see your wife nor prescribe medicine for her.

Patient: Doctor, you need not. It is not your problem.

Doctor: Now can see my next problem, I mean my patient?

Patient: I don't have any problem. But I am unable to tell you my problems that is my problem doctor. Hope you understood my real problem now.

Doctor: Sure, I understand your problem; you now may go, please.

Patient: Having taken 1000 bucks, you have not heard my problems fully, doctor.

Doctor: Ok, I give you one concession. Tomorrow evening you come once again. I will hear about your other problems without charging a consultation fee. Hope it should not be a problem for you.

Patient: No problem, is not their doctor. I fully agree to disagree with you, doctor. Hope you agree.

Doctor: I don't know what to say or do. Ok. Just check out quickly before I get into any problem with my next patient, who is already inside.

Patient: Thank you, doctor. Tomorrow evening I will come to you for the second consultation. I hope you will solve my problem. (Then he leaves, much to the relief of the doctor)

The next patient was standing inside but at the threshold of the door:

"Doctor, I have been undergoing an embarrassing problem for half an hour. I was asked to go inside by your helpdesk and I entered inside without any problem but waited for half an hour because that problematic patient was not leaving you.

Doctor: Never mind, at times such odd patients take out a hell of your time, leaving you with more problems without allowing the doctor to solve their own problems. Then, the consultation with the 3rd patient started.

Part 2

The next day, the first patient went to the doctor's clinic. The person at the Helpdesk was different from the one who was at the Helpdesk the day before.

Patient: I had my first consultation with the doctor yesterday. He could not hear my problems fully. I have been asked to come for the second consultation today.

Helpdesk: I have no problem. But the problem is the doctor is not available today.

Patient: Why, what is the problem with him?

Helpdesk: Well, yesterday out of the total three problem patients, two patients created a hell of problems for the doctor. The first problematic patient made the doctor's head reeling by bombarding problems after problem that were not his real problems.

Patient: Oh, sorry, why such problems for such a nice doctor? How about the second problem patient?

Helpdesk: The second problem patient was such a never-seen problematic person. It seems when the doctor asked him what his problem was, he caught the doctor unaware by asking what the problem with the doctor was.

Patient: Oh, it must have been a really problematic day for the doctor. How did the doctor respond?
Helpdesk: The doctor said "I don't have just one problem. I carry thousands of problems but I have never heard any of my patients asking me what my problem was."
Patient: "By the way what is the problem with the doctor, why he has not turned up today?
Helpdesk: After the second problematic patient went out of his cabin, the doctor was feeling very uneasy and sick. After interacting with yet another problematic patient, the doctor literally fainted.
Patient: "Oh, poor chap, landing into a problem while trying to solve others' problems. What happened then?"
Helpdesk: He was taken to a hospital. Doctors at the hospital diagnosed him with acute "Problimaotiatica disorder", a rare disease found in one out of one billion people. Though curable, it may take at least a week's time for total recovery, if there is no other problem or complication. The medicine seems that the word 'problem' should never be uttered in his presence. Otherwise, his health would become more problematic.
Patient: Oh, it is quite a serious problem. I have never heard of such a health disorder to date.
Helpdesk: Why the doctors in the other hospital had faced so many problems in diagnosing him and finding out about this new disease? It was only this afternoon, after a marathon Google search and lab research, they concluded about the doctor's health condition.
Patient: Will it be a problem, if I wait with my problems till the doctor recovers and comes back to the clinic?
Helpdesk: Oh, sorry, I forgot to tell you, before fainting, the doctor moaned feebly to the compounder "Never ever allow the last two patients inside the clinic. I say never and never".

Sir, now you may leave with your problems, and live with them, till our doctor recovers from his health problems.

Patient: Sure, I will never come to this problematic clinic. After all, this is not the only clinic in this big town to solve my problems. I shall search for a consultation-free and problem-free doctor to discuss my problems. I wish your doctor a speedy recovery from his present problem so as to be fit to listen to others' problems without taking others' problems as his problems.

(As the patient was leaving, the security guard rushed to the Helpdesk who became unconscious suddenly)

Thought
Oldage outage

Our teeth shrink to sweet sixteen, balance pulled out
Our vision turns bitter sixty after the cataract surgery
Our hearing sounds like a stone thrown into the well
It is difficult to detect the disorders inside our hearts
But it is easy to feel the pain in joints, kneecaps, etc.
It is not certain when bones would wear out or break
We ourselves don't know why our minds keep thinking!

Thought
Happiness in life

Birth gives life
Life gives Education

Education gives career
Career gives salary
Salary gives Money
Money gives Food
Food gives Satisfaction
Satisfaction gives contentment
Contentment gives peace
Peace gives happiness
Happiness gives life

Humour

Professor: Why English has only 26 alphabets?
Student: Who said, Sir? It has only seven alphabets, E.N.G.L.I.S.H

* * *

Student: Professor, at this young age, why do you wear spectacles?
Professor: My wife suggested I wear a zero power spectacle so that you students would treat me as a Professor.

* * *

Professor of Philosophy: Can anyone define what 'Philosophy' is?
One Student: Any opinion that won't fit in any other subject.

* * *

Student: Sir, you are teaching English subject for more than thirty years, but you have not become an English man?
Professor: You have been eating pizza since your childhood, you have not become a Pizza.

* * *

Professor: What was the difference between Queen Elizabeth and Princess Diana?
Student: Princess Diana went to a college and became a teacher, then became a global celebrity. The college went to Queen Elizabeth and made her Preacher, making her a local liability.

* * *

Student: Sir, why every student studying master's doesn't become a Professor?
Professor: Not everyone is cursed to live and die as a one-sided terrible mis-communicator.

* * *

Student: Sir, what is the difference between a lecturer and Professor?
Principal: A lecturer enjoys lecturing while a professor enjoys professing

* * *

Reporter: What is the achievement of this college, last year?
Principal: The College sent five students to NASA and five hundred students indulged in NASA (Natural Acts of Sexual Arousal)

* * *

Principal: What is your assessment of your class students?
Professor: The girl students look beautiful even if they are angry or agitated but the boy students look horrible even if they are happy and cheerful.

* * *

Thought
Feeling joy is rich

If you are born rich, you are really lucky;
If you are highly qualified, you are industrious;
If you are well employed, you are fortunate;
If you are married happily, you are a superhero;
If you are hale and healthy, you are truly wealthy;
If you are pursuing your hobbies, you are smart;
If you help others, you are a kind man;
If you help the poor, you are a nobleman;
If you have fewer expectations, you have more happiness;
If you're silent for thirty minutes a day you are resilient;
If you have a good sense of humour, you are an entertainer;
If you are not dependent on others for joy, you are great!

Thought
Love, Peace, and Joy make life's perfect triangle

Life is all that you think-a simple way life defined
Everyone's life is quite unique and is predestined
No one can compare their life, with anyone else's
Life is uncertain and mysterious-many people tell
For those with decent jobs or businesses, it's cool
Think of the poor devastated by the tyranny of life
Should not we all be thankful for our well-fed life?
Dream and toil to realize life goals, without greed

Be loyal to people with whom you are dutybound
One can't afford to be lethargic, for what we earn
Extend 'Be Active' logic at home, you can win life
We need only contentment to have peace and joy
Serve the poor as much and bid a smiling farewell

Thought
Mother-The golden feather in our life

Did she say goodbye the moment she delivered us? No
Did she feed us artificial milk when we were newborns? No
Did she give us to someone for caring and growing us? No
Did she abandon us till we grew and were able to walk? No
Did she show any discrimination among her children? No
Did she enjoy her vacation and holidays, leaving us? No
Did she sleep at all whenever we suffered from ill health? No
Did she discriminate between her good and bad offspring? No
Did she cry or complain whenever she faced life's suffering? No

She risked her life for giving life to us, she struggled to bring us up, and she sweated, unmindful of her wet eyes, to educate us, she toiled to make us complete people, and she did all these without showing any semblance of pain, agony, trouble, torture, etc. The first and best trait of every mother is they never expect anything in return from us.

Of course, in many cases, fathers too have been contributing very well in giving all support, be it financial or emotional in shaping and moulding their children. Such great fathers are also to be remembered along with the glorious mothers.

Mothers' Day is celebrated all over the world, as a symbolic gesture to the yeoman services rendered by every selfless and loving mother on earth. Otherwise, every day is a glorious Mother's Day.

Let us thank our mother for all she has done, let us keep loving her with all affection and affinity, let us vow to give our respect and protect her dignity and self-esteem at any cost, and keep her smiling till her last breath. That is the only way we can pay our gratitude to our One and only Mother, our beloved and divine mother. Cheer your mother forever!

Humour

Ramanathan: 'I remember to have seen you somewhere'.

Natharaman: 'I am your son Natharaman. I returned to India today after being away for 10 years in the US.

Gopalakrishnan: 'I am Govalakrishnan from Trivandrum'

Krishna Gopal: 'I am Krishnagoval from Suchindram'

Kalyanasundaram: 'I am Kalyanam, the son of Sundaram, hence I am Kalyanasundaram'

Sundarakalyanam: 'I am Sundaram, father of Kalyanam so I am Sundarakalyanam'

Ramasubramanian: 'My father never called me Ramasubramanian, Rama, or Subramanian. He always addressed me as 'Mottai' (which means bald-headed).

Subramanianraman: 'Me too. My father never called me Subramanian or Raman. He always addressed me as "Chottai'.

Saintsanyasi: 'I am married to two wives. But my parents kept me the name "Saintsanyasi"

Sanyasisaint: 'My father was a Sanyasi, and my mother was a Saint. They did not marry, so they kept my name as "Sanyasisaint'.

* * *

Thought
Life is nothing but what it is

What is life? I don't know
Living life with a smile makes it more pleasant
What is the purpose of life? I don't know
Living it by giving more makes the purpose easier.
What is love? I don't know
But true love has nothing to do with romance and lust
What is the need for marriage? I don't know
But marriage compels us to seek beyond the material world
What is the need for friendship? I don't know
But having even one soul mate can give great relief
What is the need for a career or business? I don't know
But by indulging in these, one can kill time and earn money
What is the need for entertainment? I don't know
But entertaining and entertainment are the best stress-busters
What is good and bad? I don't know
But living with a smile makes one feel good
In that case, one feels bad without a smile

Thought
Do it today, now, at this moment

Our normal tendency is to fulfil the obligations of enjoyment and recreation on priority. The best example is, attending social parties and get-togethers, where our role is just to participate in the celebrations and enjoy some fun time. Such occasions invariably include high-Tea, dinner, etc. not to talk of other soft drinks on certain other social and personal occasions.

But when it comes to keeping time with other essential activities like daily exercise, meditation, periodical housekeeping, servicing of our vehicles, renewal of license and other such documents, reading of books, calling on old friends, attending to defective things at home (leakage of tap, broken washroom mirror, change of lights, repair of doors, windows, etc.), the tendency is generally lazy, lethargic and procrastination.

In my 60+ years, I learned many better and bitter lessons due to having such an indifferent attitude. But ironically I continued to procrastinate some of my activities. Most of the time I ended up, paying a penalty and a heavy price for such lethargy, negligence, and procrastination. I am sure I do not have to give any examples on these accounts since everyone must have undergone such utterly bitter experiences.

I am convinced that if you want to really have a jittery-free and relieved life, please make it **a point to write down what you want to do,** say in the next couple of days or in a week's time. Please ensure that you do not jot it down on a piece of paper because the paper is either misplaced or torn into pieces or directly gets exported to a dust bin. Use a pocket diary notepad on your smartphone for jotting down the activities to be done, preferably with serial numbers, so that completed activities can be ticked or deleted later.

Keep seeing this every day, at least once, and round off the completed activities. You may also like to categorize this into urgent and others if you want to classify it on the basis of priority. You can note any damn thing and watch for yourself as to how timely, quickly, or delayed you do it. Initially, you may feel this practice a bit irksome but take it as an official meeting, that you don't like but has to be attended by you. So, start maintaining a list of 'to be completed' activities and update it. In a week or two you will appreciate the usefulness of such a list.

I guarantee this practice. It really pays rich dividends including promoting your mental and physical health by reducing the pressure and stress. You all know pretty well what I have said above but then we always like to hear good moral stories now and then either for the sake of killing time or to appreciate them or act wherever feasible. I don't know in which category you fall into.

Thought

When I was born? How long is my life, and what I should do in life?

My mortal body, I understand, was unloaded onto this planet on 17.04.1959

My immortal soul, as I understand seems to be around at all times doing fine

I express this thru my mind that too sprang along with my body on this planet
My soul, though pervading throughout my body, I find too difficult to connect
I am of the opinion one should live the life gifted by God as long as destined
I can't do anything with my life period, I arrived here with the unknown DOE
I wonder whether I really want to do anything in this cut-throat material world
I just break into joy whenever I realize I haven't thought much of getting gold
It is always my earnest prayer that everyone should have food, cloth, shelter
I look at the world and feel disheartened by the unending fights and disaster
I would like to remain calm rather than commit any act that would be harmful
I wish to be of some help to some deserving creatures, even if it is a handful
God has blessed me with food clothes, and shelter for which I am so grateful

Thought
I dream of a violence-free world

Ancient men resorted to killing animals for food. Today men fire at innocent animals to feel good. In historic times, a man killed a man as part of the war. Today a man kills another for fun and to steal cars. Fanatic Hitler went cynical, killing millions of Jews. Posterity will erase him as the most inhuman man. The founding of religions only divided the people. Forming of nations triggered a show of arrogance. Competition among the nations prompted enmity.

Thus selfishness grew among nations and people. Concurrently, the population soared exponentially. This affected countries' real growth and prosperity. Initially, violence began with the abuse of children. Jealousy failed love, and dowry abet murder acts. The violence of terrorism has no value for humans. Today the dignity of mankind is like spoiled fruit. Nature too smiles often thru catastrophic violence. Millions of cultured minds absorb these in silence. We are proud of being born in Mahatma's country. Violence will be killed if the world practices peace

Thought
Why do we get bored?

We do not like what presently we are doing. When we are in a fix- as to what to do next. Someone keeps hammering us with gossip. Lack of choice in life to enjoy the real charm. We are not happy with the people around us. We are deranged bachelors or family people. Our brains are deprived of good oxygen flow. We are compelled to do things we don't want. When we miss or misunderstand our buddies. Watching a movie for the 10th time to kill time. Lack of interesting msg on FB and WhatsApp. If someone has none of these boredom issues. They are the right people to enhance boredom.

Humour

Someone1 asked: 'Why there is a non-stop war going on between Russia and Ukraine'?
Someone2 answered: Vladimir Putin kidnapped a rabbit from the house of Ukraine's President Volodymyr Zelensky and in retaliation, Zelensky abducted a cat from the house of Putin. Putin was prepared to give a tin of whisky to Zelensky as compensation for kidnapping his rabbit but Zelensky suspected drinking that whisky was risky which he expressed openly to the press in a husky voice. On his part, Zelensky was prepared to feed milk to Putin's cat which was not acceptable to Putin because his cat never drank milk but only vodka.
Someone1???
Someone 2: Putin charged Zelensky saying "For him, it was just a cat but for me, it was my fat cat. So, right now, my position is like a cat on the wall. Later in a press conference, he told the reporters "Even though it was a cat, it never caught any rat because it was afraid of rats."
Putin later put in secretly, a word of mutual trust to Zelenskky through email wherein he (his typist) inadvertently misspelled the Ukraine President's name as 'Zelen is risky'.
Annoyed with this mail, Zelensky wanted to change his name to 'Zelen is not risky' but his wife 'Olena' said "Nothing doing. If you change your name, then I will change my name to 'Onnumillao kiski Jabardassy'. At this, Zelensky told her "Please don't do that. Already I am struggling to recall my own name. Instead, I will ask Putin to change his name to 'Dhaadisko meeshako paagalskov Katin'.
Someone1???
Someone 2: When Ukraine President suggested the Russian President change his name to "Dhaadisko meeshako paagalskov

Katin' on WhatsApp, Mr Putin reacted sharply on Facebook saying "The first two letters UK in Ukraine clearly indicate that 7654 years ago, Ukraine was part of the UK when the UK was not a part of Russia". Not stopping with this, Putin shouted in a muted voice that he would PUTIN his resignation rather than change his name. (He whispered into the ears of one one of the reporters "I am even prepared to change the name of Russia to 'Rosaiah' but not change my name).

Someone1???

Someone 2: Irked by this reaction from Mr Putin, Zelensky vented his feelings on Instagram as follows:

"Like many other rabbits, my 'Damit' (Rabbit's name) also eats carrots. But I can't eat a raw carrot but only halwa (sweet) made of carrot. If Mr.Putin is a humanitarian let him feed carrots or at least carrot halwa to Damit at least once a day. If his halwa is tasty, then Ukraine will import carrot halwa from Russia. So, it is better Mr Putin returns my Damit. "

Someone1???

Someone 2: Mr Putin did prepare carrot halwa and fed Damit, the rabbit. It liked the sweet so much that it became the pet of the Russian President. In the same way, Zelensky fed beetroot halwa to the cat and soon the cat became his pet. At the same time, both presidents wanted their original pets. This situation started worsening and lead to a feud between the two countries. That was how the tussle between the two Presidents ultimately resulted in triggering the ongoing war between these two countries. But one thing the world knows 'Putin wants to make Ukraine like a thin tin and Zelensky is bent on sitting in a revolving chair above the Russian sky'.

Suddenly, Someone1 lost his cool and slapped Someone2 somewhere on his body. Someone2 too slapped Someone1 elsewhere. At the same time, there was heavy bombing on the border. Deafened by the sound, both of them ran away in opposite directions, one toward Russia and the other toward Ukraine.

* * *

Thought
The Mood swing

Every Sunday is a gift for the working people. But all Sundays don't bring joy, a simple fact. Each Monday starts heavily in the normal course. But at times Mondays too can bring some joy. Come Friday, the charm of the weekend glows up. But not all Fridays guarantee such a big light-up. So we come to notice the thing called, mood. Due to mind upset, we say 'no' even to dude. Some angry or devil moods pop up in the mind. When things do not happen to our choice. Our mood boy inside makes flutters and noise. The more one contends, the more joy. The less one expects the fewer mood swings.

Thought
Time can change anything

We easily take negative things deep into us while at the sight of success, we lose the balance and behave egoistically. Worries and sorrows are at best treated as uninvited guests and passing clouds! Let them come and go! Whenever elated by success, money, or fame, let the humbleness in you peep out and the arrogance in you keep out! But the choice is yours! One can choose to begin as a floor cleaner and turn into a successful businessman, producing various cleaning products! One may start as a cobbler and end up as the owner of a shoe factory. It may be the other way also like someone flourishing as a textile merchant and ending up in stitching garments, someone manufacturing wine and becoming one begging for a peg of wine in a bar. Know the basic rules of the life game and deploy your intelligence and smartness to grow with your ambitions and aspirations. What you sow will grow for you either to weep or reap!

Anecdote

You must have come across a number of life instances where successful people getting ruined themselves. I had a friend, who went abroad, earned lots of money, and came back to India. He started spending lavishly on alcohol, women, and gambling. Today he has no bank balance but debts. Fortunately, he is surviving at the mercy of his son, who, in spite of knowing his father's habits, is taking care of him.

In another case, one of my relatives, who were financially sound, somehow got into horse-race betting in those days, when it was popular in Chennai in the sixties and seventies. Betting on horses, mostly unsuccessfully he ultimately lost everything and was penniless. He became a shadow of his own. So much wretched his condition was that he stopped going to his relatives and friends. Finally he along with his wife was rescued by their son-in-law who accommodated the couple in their final phase of life.

Times are never the same, so be careful at every stage
Act timely to ensure adequate corpus in your ripe age

Humour

Bolebale Balla went to a bakery and ordered a burger. While waiting he noticed the name board of the bakery wherein the words "50 years still baking" were highlighted. He thought "How many more years should I wait for my burger?" and immediately cancelled the order.

Bolebale Balla saw another bakery with the name board "Always A1- Always baked in the oven". He asked the waiter "Since how long your bakery is A1"? The waiter replied "25 years". Bolebale Balla was shocked and said "You should have scored at least A20 in this long period." He then walked away from that bakery.

Bolebale Balla walked a kilometre and found one large bakery. The name board of the bakery contained the following: "Have any worry? Don't worry. We will change it to cherry with our curry". Balla, feeling glad, went inside and told the waiter "I have one worry". The waiter asked "What is your worry?" Balla replied, "My worry is I have no worry. Change this worry into cherry and bring me curry along with two veg burgers. Hurry".

After some time a waiter came and placed two veg burgers on Balla's table. Balla asked him without looking at him "How about cherry and curry? The waiter told him "Now look up and see me ". Balla looked up. The waiter was his father. His waiter-father asked him "Now tell me what your worry is? Balla replied innocently "I don't have any cash to pay for these burgers".

* * *

Thought
Some tips for living a better life

Let the alarm bell not wake you but your peaceful sleep. Let your morning not rise after the sun but by the close of the moon. Let your face not look frown but beam a smile from the heart. Let your start not be made by cellphone but by meditation. Let your body not go with lethargy but sweating energy. Let your b/fast not so rich in fat-let it enrich your health. Let your day not open with stress but begin with trust. Let us not get stranded in traffic but reach the office in time. Let us not expect greets to reciprocate but take the lead. Let us not expect perfection in office but let's be sincere. Let us not gossip much but work reasonably to set targets. Let us not talk politics in lunch hr but have 5mts solitude. Let us not go back home cheerless but with smiling hearts. Let us not spark anger at home but illuminate it with love. Let us not carry TV news or serials to bed but ease and peace. Let us not forget to smile at people and wishing Goodnight.

Thought
Affection wins over Perfection

The moment we are born-there starts connection
When we set out for school-it is life's first injection
When we fall victim to certain things it is addiction
One wants to live as per his values and conviction
If my thoughts influence someone-it is an infection
Shining moon light up the night sky is a perfection

Mother's love and father's care showcase affection
Some dedicate more time to their work's perfection
Other relationships are not built upon any affection
But some strange associations thrive with devotion
Where one's real affection wins another's perfection

Thought
There is a limit to Tolerance and Patience

We are more than animals-satiating our needs. Animals limit themselves to acting as per their instincts. We, great humans, are the embodiment of desires. Just because we happen to have brain's faculty. We indulge too much in sins of ingenuity. We kill anything including humans just like that. Killing animals and quelling trees, we get pleasure. The irony is we preach love, non-violence, and whatnot. Humans are real hypocrites defaming humanity. Seeing the height of barbarism in this world, I wonder is there really a God with a magic wand? If he were to be here, can he be mute to evils and sins? After careful analysis, I have formed my opinion that world happenings are perhaps mystic mysteries. Maybe faith is the inevitable thread of our survival, lack of which might, perhaps stop the human revival.

Humour

English grammar teaching:
Teacher: 'I killed you". Is this in active or passive voice?

Raghu: It is a threatening voice, Sir
Teacher: No
Ramu: Is it a horrible voice Sir?
Teacher: Both are incorrect. It was my active voice

Teacher: "I need Rs.1000/- urgently", now give me its tense
Prabhu: Sorry, Sir I have only hundreds
Gopu: If I give you 10s, what will I do for evening snacks, Sir?
Teacher: Don't bother yourselves. Urgency is only in the question. You may give me Rs1000/- by tomorrow.

Teacher: I ate only eleven bananas yesterday during fasting. Is this a correct sentence?
Ravi: I don't think so Sir. How come you gave only one banana to your wife?
Prakash: Sir, you are bluffing. What you observed was not fasting but banana feasting
The Teacher writes the following on the board, Ihitmy neighbor with big wooden stickhehit me with a hockey stick my mother hit me with broomstick
Then he asks: "Insert commas and full stops at the right places"
Bharath: Only one full stop after the last stick because there is hardly any space left between the other sticks to insert either comma or a full stop.
(By the way, the above sentence is 'I hit my neighbour with a big wooden stick he hit me with a hockey stick my mother hit me with a broomstick')
Teacher: Using the phrase 'homework', give me a sentence.
Raju: I could not do my homework yesterday due to many homely works at home.

Teacher: Your answer fetches you both reward and punishment. Reward for the correct sentence and punishment for not doing the homework. Which one do you want first, reward or punishment?
Raju: Sir, I consider your reward as my punishment.

Thought
True devotion to God

We resort to many ways of worshipping the Almighty
Visiting many temples and praying for our prosperity
We pray to numerous deities in temples and at home
Recite devotional hymns, songs, and chanting of Aum
Devotees sing many bhajans in and outside the home
We believe and claim, whatever happens, is His's will
Without clear introspection, we live amidst many evils
If all our acts happen by the will of the omnipotent God
Then why the unending miseries that hurt us very hard
I believe that our acts in earlier births influence this life
God is just an invisible power that can give us strength
So that one could face the suffering and grief of this life
Hence, total dependence on God is not a wise thinking
Live with courage, trust yourself, and be your own king

Thought
Dusserah, an opportunity to give

Come Dusserah! We go about creating a special fund
To facilitate meeting gratis and gifts to workers around

The milk delivery boy is the first person we meet daily
Give him a small bonus and make him feel joy and jolly
Paperboy at times overtakes the milk boy with hot news
Pass on some bonus to him, maybe you get good news
The servant maid shows up every day during the week
Gift her at least a new sari or else you will feel so sorry
Do not undermine the watchman and his watchwoman
A decent bonus and sari to them can bring good omen
Tip the garbage picker who ensures your place is clean
He enables you to keep your place healthy and hygiene
You may curb certain other expenses but not the above
Dusserah is the time to give them what they need more

Humour
Brain Sprain

A muscular sprain is a known health problem that occurs when contraction in muscles results in pain. Throat pain is a known feature with many, where inflammation in the throat causes pain. Dental pain is so common with large people, where decay or infection in teeth results in pain. Stomach pain seems to exist since Stone Age, which features pains due to indigestion, irregular bowl movements, gas formation inside, etc.

Knee pain has come to remain a life disorder. Knee caps wearing out, incapacitating walk and strain to the knee caps. Chest pain is common and universal in India. Varying pains felt due to heart deficiencies. But friends, have you heard of brain sprain? To put it simply, it is a sprain in the brain. There is good news about this brain sprain. This sprain troubles only those with a brain. Especially those who use brains beyond 24/7. Brain sprain occurs when the brain lacks humour. The periodical feeling of humour keeps the brain fine. Avoid laughing at people but laugh at yourself. Laughing bellyful reduces brain sprain by half. Researchers at No-Brain University now say that more than 100% of males get brain sprains. The brains of 278.5 males were tested at the No-Brain lab. Only females are permitted and are equipped to carry out brain tests at this lab. Ms.Femaly Brainy, the youngest female but the most senior researcher at No-Brain lab says "This is the only lab in the entire world, researching the strains in the brain caused by brain strain. Of the 337.75 adults, mostly males, tested for brain strains, 53.97% have expressed lesser satisfaction about their brains. 19.76% were unable to express anything clearly as their brains were completely drained after the initial dosage of brain-suppressing pills. The remaining adults were unable to express clearly what is what, although they have working brains. So we can say that the study has successfully showcased the negative brains of the males, under certain given conditions. However, our next course of research is to study the performance of brains under certain not given conditions".

Last month I was selected on a random basis to go to their lab for undergoing brain strain.

I am glad to share with you that I am lucky, to have been diagnosed with a brain Sprain.

My brain in soft copy is in the No-Brain lab now. Now I am convinced that I too have

BRAIN. However, the final results on brain sprain for the select males will be out only after the brain-storming at No-Brain University during the upcoming Brain-train-strain Conclave.

* * *

Thought (In Acronym)
Even if late, realize and internalize

Right from birth life teaches, which are like precious stones
Every stage is marked by either pelted stones or milestones
Anyone who grasps vital lessons early is poised for success
Laziness to pick up the right threads denies the right access
Invariably people stumble in life and get hurt more than often
Zeal and will for improvement keep the doors of victory open
A man who learns, and moulds from his past succeeds better
The irony is most people repeat mistakes and feel the bitter
It is common to see people regret their past acts and deeds
One wonders, why we don't sow early the realization seeds
Never regret, leave the past, live the present, love yourself

Thought
Anything that is not material is not realistic

Anything, non-materialistic may not be really realistic
But things of spirituality are cosmic as well as mystic
How to know that something is certainly spiritualistic?

Things that give a blissful feeling that is the yardstick
Spirituality and materialism can't be bonded by plastic
As long as one keeps a bank account it is materialistic
A person with a spirituality account is the least egoistic
Where spirituality befriends materiality, it turns chaotic
A social man learning spirituality is but an enthusiastic
Trying spiritualism while pursuing materialism is idiotic

Humour
In a police station

A person barges into a police station.
Person: "I want to file an FIR"
Inspector asks, "What is the problem?"
Person: "The problem is not there now".
The inspector, puzzled by this exclaims: "When there is no problem, where is the question of filing FIR?"
Person: "My girlfriend who has been a problem to my wife, died in her house, apparently due to an allergic attack".
The inspector, getting more confused, asks him: "How are you sure that it was an allergic attack?"
Person: "My wife, who is an allergic patient, was with my girlfriend before she died."
The inspector, feeling the stars' vision inside his eyes asks "How do you know that your wife was with your girlfriend at the time of death?"
Person: At that time I was with my girlfriend
The inspector, getting charged, asks: How come your wife spared you?

Person: I am not a problem to her
Inspector: What is your age?
Person: Eighty
Inspector: What is your wife's age?
Person: Ninety
Inspector: And your ex-girlfriend's age?
Person: Hundred
Inspector: Run away from here before I count a hundred.

* * *

Thought
Meditation is not anyone's cakewalk

Have you ever sat alone in a place of silence (it could be your home or any other place for that matter), closing your eyes and observing just your breath or point of meditation for ten minutes or more? During these times, could you remain focused on your point of meditation without any distraction of thoughts in your mind? If your answer is NO, then you are the perfect one to practice meditation.

Over more than two decades, I have grappled with a few meditation techniques. Of course, not more than that. After long trial and error, I have now zeroed in on meditation which is simple but not so easy to do. It is meditating on your breathing. To get convinced of this method, it took me years of the other methods, to which I was initiated. One of the meditations emphasized observing one's thoughts without getting entangled with such thoughts. The other method is focusing on a certain figure or object and meditating on the same object or figure.

To be honest, I find the going rather very tough. I admit that barring a few rare occasions of a few seconds of deep observation of my breathing, I could not accomplish any noticeable progress or improvement in my meditation. Before proceeding further, I have to convey one most important pre-requisite for meditating. It is about having a good sleep. Not only meditation, nothing for that matter can be interesting and involving without having a good sleep. So, note this cardinal rule that good sleep alone gives the right energy to pursue any meaningful activity, and meditation is no exception. A sound sleep alone can facilitate you to take up any purposeful meditation.

Practice, practice, practice

One can wield command and may afford to control anything outside, whether it is people or circumstances. But it is the last thing for anyone to rein in one's mind. The mind monkey (MM) is the most startling and awesome inbuilt invisible mechanism that never rests even for a fraction of a second. Mind is relatively at rest with those few who are more illiterate or innocent, carrying the least inhibitions and reservations.

For the rest of the others, it is like a hell of a time, beaten, shaken, jolted, grilled, squeezed, pierced, punished, bombarded, etc by their mind. Such is the enormity of the mind's thinking. On any given day, an average person's mind is engulfed and inundated by heaps of peeping, sweeping, beeping, and weeping thoughts. So much so that one doesn't even know what he is thinking unless one pauses deliberately and keenly watches his mind. With such a mind of a chaotic environment, meditating peacefully is the most stupendous task.

Focus; concentrate on your meditation with all your determination. You keep thinking, worrying, etc digressing from the object of meditation. Every time when you are able to observe that you are deviating, realign your focus and continue. Still, you end up observing a plethora of thoughts encircling in your mind. Again take a deep breath and plunge into meditation. Soon the uninvited guests of thoughts enter your mind rather more vigorously. You feel distracted and again counsel yourself to be stronger, point-focused and stay on course and then continue with meditation. Alas, in no time, you are battered by fresh or repetitive thoughts. One is awed by the never-ceasing thought waves and the distraction they cause in the process of meditation.

By sitting in solitude and meditating every day, relentlessly, earnestly with a sense of purpose one will find in oneself a change, however subtle it may be. That will be a change, that gives the

Feeling that one has improved over his past self.

Thought
Love is beyond affection

Real affection is giving without an iota of inhibitions
True friendship is not letting down one's friend ever
Divine love is loving the other without expectations
Noble charity is giving without expecting a publicity
Gentlemanship is behaving pleasantly with all alike
Pristine love is pure compassion not person biased

Thought
I am a representative of Humour

The pace of my humour is fast
The space of my humour is vast
I will live joyfully till I exist and
I will leave gracefully when I exit
I know there are crooked means
To me, it means poisoned beans
I know what is happening to me
But I don't know why it happens
I do make others smile and laugh
Hardly a few only could reciprocate

Thought
Breath life slowly, walk it lively

Breathe life with the two lungs of healthy thoughts and cleanliness!
Inhale the healthy and worthy things, exhale stale and filthy things!
Look at life with sharp eyes of moral courage and practical wisdom!
Listen to life's live voice with keen ears of silence and awareness!
Handle the life blows with the strong hands of truth and confidence!
Kick every trouble with the dashing legs of super will and resilience!

Give back to life by living with compassion and a nature-loving pal!
Talk about life's beauty with a mint-munching mouth of enthusiasm!
Execute the duties of life with a sense of honesty and commitment!
Walk on its road of ups and downs like a majestic walking elephant!

It is me and my Destiny

Time, since my birth, time, and again, spoiled my time!
Circumstances, unfair in many situations, betrayed me!
People, from all walks of my life, walked away from me!
Opportunity grabbed my opportunities and cheated me!
Friends, right from my childhood, misbehaved with me!
Sleep often woke me up in the night and punished me!
Holistic health is thrilled playing hide and seek with me!
Destiny in my every destination, provoked and hurt me!
But I never stop, giving these mad fellows a tough fight

Thought
Unkempt nails and unnoticed paradise

A jogging shoe pair could be lost due to the unkempt foot nails
A sharp-edged scissor could become blunt due to rust forming
A rich blazer could become a rag due to negligence in ironing
A good relative might be lost due to a long communication gap
A close friendship could break away due to a misunderstanding

A married couple may divorce due to differences in tiny matters
A precious time is lost when the past is lamented in the present
All hell breaks loose due to not realizing the paradise on hand

Thought
What you are

What you say is right if you say it simple and straight
What you do is correct if what is done is transparent
What you think is fine if your consciousness is in line
What you're is great if you don't care how others rate

Thought
It is City Vs Sity

Want to have great materialistic times? Stay in any Megacity
Want to feel how you feel without electricity? Switch off Electricity
Want to confront a notorious bad element? Have the Audacity
Want to have a doctorate in some subject? Enrol in a University
Want to help as many deserving people? Know your capacity
Want to be a leader of any forum or party? Develop Sagacity
Want to experience how horrible life is? Undergo Adversity
Want to enjoy the sensuous luxuries in life? Invite Prosperity
Want to keep learning one or the other? Have the Curiosity
Want to appreciate how happy life is? Embrace Simplicity

Thought
Many faces of money

She is the mother who loves ever you but never money
He is a proud father only when you work and earn money
She is an adorable wife as long as you keep giving money
He is your elder brother as long as you don't seek money
He is your younger brother if you could extend him money
She is your elder sister whenever you greet her with money
She is your younger sister if you give her in kind or money
He is just a friend who keeps clinging to your rope of money
He is a true friend who can forego sleep to get you money!

Thought
Valentine's Day

India, a long time ago was culturally glorious and spiritually pristine!
Life had the best standards made from the rich knowledge of turpentine!
But foreign invasions distorted us and forced us into a slavery quarantine!
Earlier, on this day, youth pairs used to line up in the parks in serpentine!
Today's youth value the values and dispel the wrong notions of Valentine!

Thought
Life is a week

If Monday is a Child
Tuesday is an Adult
If Wednesday is Romance
Thursday is Marriage
If Friday is Employment
Saturday in Retirement
If Sunday is expiry,
Carry and bury on Monday

Thought
India Vs US-China and Russia

The US is ever-clamouring to preach to the rest of the world
China is greedy ever-ready to dominate the rest of the world
Russia is ever-anxious to invite the attention of the world
India is ever-silent setting an example to the entire world!
Habits die hard

Thought
Millionaires have plenty, so plenty of poor

While we are relaxing with a cup of hot tea, there are millions whose purses are empty;

When we are enjoying an evening at a party, there are numerous who are fighting poverty;
When we are happily rejoicing in our homes, lakhs of people perish and die on the streets;
Is love meant only for our family? Is not universal love, in rescuing the poor from starving?
Is service working for employers' salary? Is it not for servicing the poor without any fees?
Is humanity the world's human community? Or in being kind and giving in kind to the poor?

Thought
Don't entertain anything past

The deadly nature of the mind is rewinding the past
The critical habit of memory is the recall of the past
Whether rewind or recall, the past is simply a waste
Sweet it's rosy like patches but hurting its scratches
Appreciating this simple fact, make your mind alert
Live like the running river that remains clear of dust

Thought
Can we stop killing animals?

A fish in the aquarium is a pet but the fish everywhere else is food, why?
A chicken running around its mother looks cute but later becomes food, why?

A lamb is played with, like a pet but sooner or later it turns into food, why?
A pig is shunned as the filthiest animal but it is delicious as pork, why?
A cow is the friend of humans but it is inhumanly slaughtered for food, why?
All humans are supposed to love but many feasts on the killed creatures, why?
The human race can win any race but never could win over violence, why?
Because 'God is love is only in books but in practice, we kill animals at will

Humour
Request to commit silly mistakes to quench my quest

Hi dear fellow Silly Mistakeans!
It is my great blood pressure to be partially and wholly part of you, Silly Mistakeans, Mr and Mrs as well as Miss. Hope you too will have high blood pressure like me on reading this massage like a gentle massage. The mistake is a privilege at any age. Engage in and manage it. Mistakes are committed at a young age, middle age as well as old age. You notice that age is common for all the above three categories. But the prerequisite for mistakes is they should be silly. I am sure you all are not so silly that you don't understand what is silly. In case you have any doubt about what is silly, immediately consult your friend Lilly. If your silly mistakes lack humour, then, add some chilly. Mind you that the readers should be able to laugh from their

belly, on noticing your silly mistakes. Wish you manipulate and manifest yourself with as many silly mistakes.
With a great volley of silly comments
Silly Mistakean with the surname 'Pulley'

* * *

Thought
Can knowledge give happiness?

One who is an academic scholar wants to flaunt his knowledge
One who inherited fortunes and riches wants to showoff wealth
One blessed with artistic skills is eager to exhibit them in public
One who doesn't possess anything significant keeps gossiping
One who is selfless presses themselves for serving the weaker
One who can't create their own thoughts forwards others' stuff
One who is contented and happy thinks about others' welfare!

Thought
Disenchanted, so what?

My childhood was devoid of play and fun, but I was a child nevertheless!
My school days were dull and mechanical, but I was a student all right!
My youth began like a butterfly and ended like a bitter fly but still, I flew!

My career was copious rainfall in the forests, but nothing short of money!
My life has been a paradise of scars and a hell of joys but still, it is a life!
My times jerk me quite often but my life mantra is Live your moment lively!

Humour

1. Friend 1: What did you pray at the temple?
2. Friend 2: For my remarriage
3. Friend 1: what happened to your first wife?
4. Friend 2: She is already remarried

* * *

5. 2. Friend 1: What is the secret of your 50 years of married life?
6. Friend 2: Daily we sleep in two bedrooms
7. Friend 1: Great, how do you sleep together in two bedrooms daily? How far is it practicable?
8. Friend 2: No, we sleep separately in two bedrooms.
9. Friend 1: Hope you are having wonderful times after marriage.
10. Friend 2: Your statement is like asking a blind person 'Are you enjoying the beauty of nature'?
11. Friend 1: Who is that lady who has been dancing so energetically with those six men?
12. Friend 2: She is celebrating her sixth successful divorce event with her ex-husband.

* * *

13. Friend 1: What do you do for your livelihood, now that you are not working in Bollywood?
14. Friend 2: I give paid counselling to people in my neighbourhood to explore the vast avenues awaiting them in Hollywood.

* * *

Thought
Think twice before quitting any friendship or relationship

We look at people from our perception and outlook. If the other person matches with some qualities we have, we consider them as good But, if the other person gets into any confrontation or difference of opinion, we brand them as bad, momentarily forgetting the fact that except for certain aspects of their behaviour, they are good otherwise.

For example, the other person may be having the attitude to help the poor and needy but gets into heated arguments with others on certain issues and may even hurt their feelings in the process. Afterwards, he may brush aside such incidents and behave friendly. But due to our egoist nature, we chose to avoid them and even eliminate their association. It will be only wise and prudent to forget and forgive the other person for his negative stance on certain stand-alone issues and see him in totality. I am a good example of this aspect. I had cut off many people from my life due to my not liking them for their certain actions or behaviour, without analyzing and appreciating the other person as a whole.

At times, I feel and regret that I behaved irrationally in haste and was overwhelmed by the momentary rupture created in me, without taking into account the other person's overall traits. We know for certain that every person has good and bad traits. As long as we are able to appreciate his positive aspects, why eliminate him for the sake of one instance of his indifferent behaviour? Can we confess that we are divine-like persons, without any negative qualities in us?

It pays if we get along with people, without minding so much about their negative aspects, as long as we are not really affected by such negativities.

Anecdote

Thirty years back, I visited one of my distant relatives. Just then, he took voluntary retirement from his organization. I was in my late twenties. He liked me and I too reciprocated. He had a practical outlook on life. He suggested useful life tips. I must have visited time three or four times.

Once, it so happened, I invited him to the housewarming ceremony of my new flat. Due to some other reason, he could not attend the function. I took it so personally that I kept him at a distance after this event. It is almost thirty years and my relative is still alive. But practically I lost touch with him. In fact, he once visited my house two decades ago along with my maternal uncle, without grudging about my attitude towards him. But even then, I continued to maintain a hard stance with him. When my mother passed away about seven years ago, he did not make any inquiry, although he visited her on earlier occasions. I took this as another opportunity to keep him away.

With my above uneasy experience, in my life-kitty, I suggest the readers be more mature, sensible, and practical while looking at the other person with contempt. Being emotional and over-sensitive brings only negative results and won't serve the purpose.

It is child's play to cut friendships like plucking a flower
Restoring friendship ties would be like building fly-over

Humour
The Left over Right definitions

An engineer is the non-entity offspring of the ever-growing mind-boggling chemistry between historic science and geographical technology!

* * *

A doctor is a medicine produced with the collaboration of many senior doctors and huge money, in order to facilitate him to explore as many money patients, till the expiry of money or patient whichever is earlier!

* * *

A lawyer is the brand ambassador of the dynamic modern truth, where the definition of truth keeps changing in proportion to the quantum of legal fees!

* * *

An honest man (if there is there anyone), is the most idiotic and impractical person who, although lured by the sweet pull of money, manages to survive by sticking to ethics!

&&&

A true human being is an extinct creature that was believed to have existed on earth amidst the other people, till India attained independence!

Thought
We laugh only to cry

While entering this world, we cry and others laugh
While leaving this world, people cry to conceal laugh
While entering the school we are afraid of teachers
When we enter college, lecturers are afraid of us!
When we finish education, we begin earning
When earning-career is over we start learning!
When we get married, our aim is sheer enjoyment
When we become parents, enjoyment forgets us!
When we have sound health, everything seems good
When age and ill health creep in everything looks bad!
While living we are carried away by some nuisance
When we croak we are carried away by ambulance!

Humour
My little Ox-Bored Dixon-Harry

Underground

A pickpocket is one who pickpockets those without right and left pockets.

A robber is one who robs those who are not heartthrobs but who have wardrobes.

A thief is one who indulges in mischievous deeds if he has his handkerchief.

A stealer is one who steals everything that has no seal, without any ceiling.

A dacoit is one who gets his DA by decamping with the day's booty and dumping it under his cot with a sense of duty.
A fraud is one who defrauds by sharpening his broad secret rod without using any sword, either owned or borrowed.

Police station

A constable is one, who is constantly stable when there's no trouble.
A policeman is one, who lies to others ' Hey man, pole is a hole'.
An inspector is one who is an inside spectator without his pet.
A commissioner is one with a mission to commission every omission without submission.

Government

A president is one, who presides over the press meets without setting any precedence, avoiding prudence.
A prime minister is one, who is primarily not Mini's sister but secondarily a mini sinister.
A minister is one, who celebrates mini Easter on many days in the east side of the West.
A Governor is one, who goes ever after some honour or dishonour, over and over.
A secretary is one who is scared with his airy appraisal of secrets that are always known to others.

University

A chancellor is one, who, given the chance, lives in his cellar with a cell.
A vice-chancellor also lives in a cellar with another cell that is vice.

A dean is one whose DNA is juxtaposed where 'e' is superfluously not silent.
A professor is one who professes without a scissor and confuses with more errors.
A lecturer is one who causes a fracture due to a lacklustre lecture, true to his nature.

Thought
Less repentance, more contentment

Even if God were to incarnate as a human being, he would have regrets and repentance. One thing for certain is that one cannot afford to postpone the present happiness. If one attempts to defer happiness for a future date, chances are that he will end up with lesser happiness or no happiness at all. Sooner on becoming an adult, one normally attempts to fulfill one's genuine desires, to the extent possible.

One need not make a big fuss about tasting alcohol or having a few puffs from a cigarette; dating with a girl or boyfriend is fine, as long the two have mutual faith and understanding. Do not try to suppress your small and reasonable desires. Give vent to them wherever opportunity permits. Suppose you want to talk to your neighbours, just do it, don't hesitate. If the neighbour likes it or encourages it, maintain the friendship, or else just leave it.

If you want to enjoy an outing with friends, go out and enjoy. If you want to learn some fine art, learn it within the time and monetary constraints. But never let your desires die a slow death. Keep doing something so that you derive the little pleasures of life. It is desired, accumulated over the period, unfulfilled, that creates a big void in your mind that has the power to revolt at the later stages in life. The pricking of disappointments and a sense of failure over these unfulfilled desires can be deeply painful and hurting.

In other words, whatever you wanted to indulge in but could not due to your reservations and inhibitions, can create mental turbulence when you become old. As a man who has undergone the above mental agony, I feel empowered to suggest you, if not advice, to tick as many desires as possible without procrastination. But never forget the watchword "Think twice before you act". It goes without saying that our acts should not hurt either ourselves or others. Make sure that you are left with the least unfulfilled desires. It is a fact that every individual, however rich or saintly he or she may be, has some regrets in life.

If small desires could not be fulfilled, one regrets it!
If it is life's burning desire one laments and repents!

Humour

Alfred Einstein was a great scientist, me a sweet humourist!

Bernard Shaw was a brilliant satirist, me a valiant re-tirist

Charlie Chaplin was an adorable comedian, me a durable Indian

Donald Bradman was a glorious cricketer, me a humourous writer

Edmund Hillary was the first to scale Everest, I am the second while taking a rest

Florence Nightingale was 'The lady with a lamp', me a daddy with a night lamp
George Washington was the first president of the US, I, a resident in the GS (Ground stairs)
Hussein Bolt was the fastest sprinter, my laser printer prints faster than a sprinter
Isaac Newton defined laws of motion; I am confined due to a lot of emotion!

* * *

I went to a place yesterday. That took place about one day ago. I shall be going to another place tomorrow. That will take place after today.
Today I am not going to any place. That is taking place today. So going to a place may or may not take place. But yesterday, today and tomorrow always take place.
To illustrate this point, Thursday takes place after Wednesday. Friday takes place before Saturday. Sunday takes place only after Saturday. But nobody else takes place their place.
In a nutshell, plays can take place in any place. But a place cannot take the place of plays.
After reading this, hope you don't misplace your mind after it gets displaced.

Thought
Sustaining the decisions to change

The most rampant quality of humans is the tendency not to change with the changes. Once you are into a certain routine or habituated to a certain style of life, it is all the more difficult to put yourself in the loop line from the main track. Classic examples are our food habits, time-passing habits, sleeping habits, and of course the grand New Year resolutions that always remain without solutions but nevertheless make it to the top spot on 31st December of every year.

Similarly, we go to places of worship and pray for making certain changes in our attitude, life routine, etc. We also hear sermons, and preaching from various religious people and other thinkers. We read various books on personality development, we attend training programs where tips for changing our lifestyle and habits for improving our overall personality are given which are very meticulously noted either in mind or note. But seldom are they put to practice due to the law of "take it easy" that is operative in every human being. So it is the question of getting convinced about certain changes we want to make in ourselves and putting into practice such change.

At times we also observe some short-term miracles by starting to change dramatically but only for a short while. In a matter of days and not even weeks, the changes contemplated slowly exit even without our knowledge and we find one fine morning with our original mindset. This phenomenon is also very common among people. But most of the time, it is the fixed notion in mind that prevails over flexibility. That is why understanding and appreciating changes is not the question. It is the willingness to accept the change and adapt oneself to put it into practice. Not only that, the crucial thing is to sustain the change from days to weeks to months to years. If one can break the jinx here, then development and growth can go hand in hand with such people. After appreciating and accepting the change contemplated, it calls for tremendous determination to change, the willpower to execute the change, and the dedication to sustain such change.

* * *

Humour

I went to Norway, situated far away on a highway built in a novel way; there is no such beautiful country, no way, I say.
I saw Sweden, it is better than any garden in London, not a burden like Biden, Wow, well done.
I visited Finland which is not an island nor a financial land but just a fine land.
I stayed in Denmark; my remark is, they use no bookmark to earmark that is their hallmark, so I give it Fullmark.
I travelled in France, and my inference is, it is full of dance and romance without any need for common sense.
I roamed in Italy which is full of valleys, here they don't use the 'tally' software to tally the good and bad, nor organize any rallies but strangely they are jolly people, really, who never wake up early.
I strained my spine due to a sprain while in Spain, and suffered with pain but ultimately due to a downpour of rain and some food grain, I recovered to gain back my original spine which is now doing fine.

* * *

The best place to eat is in a relative's marriage. One pays for one day (gift) and eats for three days.
Don't think that only the dogs on the streets bark at you. Many dogs from inside the houses, bark more furiously, either with or without the "Beware of dogs" signboard outside.
In big gatherings of the audience, when the speaker refers to some as fools, many look around to ensure that others don't look at them.
If you successfully fail to make it onto the stage, you would have succeeded in failing at that stage.

A best friend is one who takes the worst from you and still runs to you to help when you are in distress, the worst friend is one who runs away from you, after taking the best from you.

Thought
It is difficult to crack life but it is worth it

Life is clever and tricky you can't escape from it
Right from birth till death we have to live with it
While young we need work or business to live it
In middle age, family responsibilities decorate it
At the age of sweet sixty, we try to understand it
From sixty we inspect life and introspect about it
We realize and regret, we did not really utilize it
We draw solace from our certain good acts in it
Whether a pauper or king, everyone is part of it
Many of you, in young and middle age, look at it
With this insight, you will admire life and thank it

Humour

Transient global amnesia (Temporary memory loss)

Linda Nomemoria: Who are you and what the hell you're doing here?
Banta Somaniya: Hey, Linda, don't be kidding, tell me what you want to eat.

Linda Nomemoria: I want to go to the church immediately. Father will be waiting for me.
Banta Somaniya: Your father passed away last year, don't you remember?
Linda Nomemoria: He passed by this restaurant just now. He wants me to read Bible in the church.
Banta Somaniya: Come on Linda darling, be serious
Linda Nomemoria: Are you a senseless madcap, I am not your darling. Don't enrage me.
Banta Somaniya: Honey, last week we went to Darjeeling, have you forgotten darling?
Linda Nomemoria: Honey, I have many; keep them with you. I have my cousin's brother working as a bureaucrat in the court of Venice city within the province of Darjeeling.
Banta Somaniya: Oh, God, something went wrong, terribly.
Linda Nomemoria: Yes, Terrible Tandon also works with him.
Banta Somaniya: Come on Linda dear, just be cool, yesterday we went to the sea-less beach, now you remember?
Linda Nomemoria: But I went with my grandfather to the shoreless sea beach. He got me, three big cones of ice cream.
Banta Somaniya: oh, damn it, I got you two cups of ice cream yesterday. One vennila and one pista. How could you pretend to forget that, my sweetheart?
Linda Nomemoria: Vennila and Pista are my cousins. Don't drag them into our issues.
Banta Somaniya: Now, just relax, have this tomato soup.
Linda Nomemoria: Even donkeys like tomato soup
Banta Somaniya: But I don't like it.
Linda Nomemoria: That's none of my lookouts. Now tell me who you are.
Banta Somaniya: I am your romantic lover, and you are mine.

Linda Nomemoria: Nonsense, you seem to be a lunatic nut. I don't have any lover. I love only my mother.

Banta Somaniya: Well, no harm in loving your mother. But our love is something special.

Linda Nomemoria: I don't understand even a bit of your puffed-up statements. What special you are goading about?

Banta Somaniya: Two days back, we spent the night together at my house.

Linda Nomemoria: Two days ago I was not even born.

Banta Somaniya: Don't test my patience baby. We in fact slept together.

Linda Nomemoria: For the last three days I have not slept at all. If I had slept, it would have been with my dog only.

Banta Somaniya: Thank God, now, you got it right. It was me that night.

Humour
Dos and Don'ts for 2024

Dos

1. Set daily alarm @4am. But keep the alarm sound mute.
2. To sip more morning hot coffee, here is a tip: Instead of reading daily news after coffee, read it while sipping coffee.
3. Daily perform physical exercise to stay fit. Whenever your mood doesn't permit, do it mentally but briskly.
4. Always make it a point to help others by drinking and partying at their expense.

5. If you look beautiful, you have done the right makeup. If don't look beautiful, even after the makeup, something is wrong in the beholders' eyes.

Don'ts

1. Your sleep is your prerogative. Never allow others to sleep on your behalf.
2. Breakfast is the topmost meal on any day. Have it without a break, even if you had to fast on any day.
3. Doing your daily duty must be at the top of your priority list. Whenever you don't want to do your duty, remove it from the priority list.
4. Don't weep when someone hurts you. Apply ointment where it hurts.
5. Never skip any meeting, where eating follows the meeting. If eating is prior to the meeting, never skip the meeting without eating.

Thought
The daily drink called 'confidence'

Get up with cheers! Fresh up with enthusiasm! Dress up with a smile! Startup with greets! Pick up the day's momentum with huge confidence! Confidence is not exactly in having courage and guts. It is the degree of reliability in oneself while dealing with people and situations as part of one's career, profession, business, and personal life. Having courage and guts boost one's confidence level.

It is the confidence that protects one from being bullied down, from getting buried by the worried thoughts, from feeling inferior, from being criticized from feeling rejected and frustrated. It is like our daily drinks and beverages like water, coffee tea, etc. Like you drink these drinks, top up your confidence as many times during a day. But one precludes confidence is preparedness. One must have command or control over the issues to be confronted for the day. Since confidence without knowledge or understanding is like growing a plant passionately without pouring water. Knowledge, no doubt, breeds confidence and confidence can breed power. But knowledge does not automatically make one confident. It is the self-belief and trust in one's knowledge, abilities, and talents that promote confidence in a person. So, keep updating with your areas of specialization or interest so that you reap the best with your well-built confidence.

Humour
In a multistoried apartment

Visitor: I want to visit Mr Mabbu of C block.

Security, after verifying the records: There is no Mabbu in the C block.

Visitor: I visited him last month also. I think his flat no is 16.

Security: There are four 16s in this block South, North, East, and West.

Visitor: I am not sure whether it is East or West. It is somewhere between these two.

Security: In that case, it could be between North and South also.
Visitor: There is a swimming pool in front of Mabbu's flat.
Security: We have two swimming pools one in the North and another in the West.
Visitor: The swimming pool I am talking about is very small. It may be for children.
Security: The children's swimming pool is in B block.
He verifies B-16 details and informs the visitor: There is one M. Subbu in B-16. Opposite his flat, there is one small swimming pool.
Visitor: But the name appears to be wrong. My client is Mabbu not Subbu. Maybe M. Subbu stands for Mabbu Subbu. Please check.
Security, after verifying the details: He is not Mabbu Subbu but Makku Subbu.
Visitor: Then he is not my client. Mr Mabbu looks very fair, with curly hair, a small moustache, medium size nose, and big eyes.
Security: Oh, big eyes, there are twenty residents here who have big eyes. Out of that twelve are ladies. I hope your client is not a lady.
Visitor: I told you it is Mr Mabbu which means he is a male. I know he is a male married to a female. I think he has one boy and one daughter.
Security: This information is very vague. Most of the residents here have two children, one boy, and one daughter.
Visitor: Mabbu's daughter's name is Teju.
Security: Even, my own daughter's name is alsoTeju, and her actual name is Tejaswini. My boy's name is Teja.

Visitor: I am not sure about Mabuu's son's name. His wife's name starts with A.
Security, after checking the details: There are 127 women in this apartment with names beginning with A.
Visitor: Oh, then it will be very difficult to make out. Ok. Shall I give Mr Mabbu's phone number?
Security: No need, you can call him and tell him to speak with security.
The visitor then telephones Mr Mabbu: I am Babbu, LIC agent. You wanted me to visit you. What is your flat number?
Mr. Mabbu: Oh, only last month I rented out my flat to one Mr. M. Subbu and shifted to another apartment, Mount Abu Towers. It is a pretty bigger apartment compared to my earlier apartment with one thousand five hundred houses, located just opposite my earlier apartment. You come to the security via the main road which will be about three KM. I will inform security to let you inside. My flat is on the third block, in the first row, opposite to Senior Citizen block; the west wing of the North side, the flat is on the 8th floor, with invisible doors. You have to press the secret code which is 000 followed by my PAN number which I will SMS you now. Then my door will become visible and then open. You have to enter within three seconds, failing which the door will close automatically. It will not open again in the next fifteen minutes. So be quick and alert. Oh, unfortunately, the four lifts are under break down, due to strike by the lift operators and the backup is also under break down due to a cut down in diesel.
So have your breakfasts first and then come to my apartment, and climb the stairs. Don't forget to enter my flat within three seconds. I will receive you at the entrance of my flat.

The LIC agent Babbu faints. (Before fainting, he verifies whether his own LIC policy is alive on that date).

Thought
How about making the days charmingly satisfying?

Let not the alarm bell wake you up but your peaceful sleep!
Let it dawn not with the sun's rise but with the moon's set!
Let your face not be frown but beam with a smile from the heart!
Let your day begin not with the cell phone but with being alone!
Let your body not remain lethargic but sweat with exercise!
Let the breakfast be not fatty but nutritious, high in protein!
Let your day not kick start with stress but with hopes, and trust!
Let us not get upset by the snarling traffic but set up control!
Let us not wait to reciprocate others' wishes but be the first!
Let us not expect 'all is well outside' but manage, being cool!
Let us avoid gossip but work smartly to fulfil the set target!
Let us not talk debate politics but relax ourselves comfortably!
Let us not talk politics to relax but observe our mind's charge!
Let us not take stress to our home but only snacks and smile!
Let us not emit any anger at home but illuminate with cheer!
Let us not carry cell phones to bed but only peace prayers!
Let us not forget to wish our dear one a good night and sleep!

Humour

During childhood I used to crave toffee; now I crave coffee too.

I liked Geography during my school days; now I have been scripting my biography.

My main attraction during adulthood was cinema; presently my attraction is not seeing cinema.

Giving nicknames was one of my naughty activities even as a schoolboy; later I came to know that I myself had many nicknames, like mottai (bald-headed), milkman, madcap, lamboo, etc.

I truly had many close friends; Why because all those friendships were close (d).

* * *

Thought
Read it, do it, or leave it

Water is scarce and precious, save it
Power is dearer, make the least use of it
Money is endless, earn don't chase it
Gossiping is not welcome act avoid it
Anger is harmful, artfully prevent it
Hatred is anti-love; stay away from it
Helping is wonderful, do and enjoy it
Smile enhances your beauty, spray it
Laughter boosts health, do not lock it

Prayer world- welfare is selfless say it
Reading these lines is easy to practice it

Humour

Are we useful to the earth? Yes, by walking on Earth from all sides, we ensure the Earth doesn't fall from its place into the moon and crush it.

Is nature useful to us? Yes, by protecting us with solid mountains, seas, and oceans, deep forests, it ensures we stay safe within the earth's limits without falling from it to Mercury or Venus.

Are Earth and nature useful to us? No, by living on this pleasures-yielding planet and enjoying the scenic and serene beauty of nature, we crave to live longer and longer, making the newcomers to earth, suffocate and struggle for their survival.

Thought
A thunder without splendour

I lived as a child; but without pleasant memories;
My childhood was neither mild nor wild!
I lived as a student; I was devoid of enthusiasm;
I was neither prudent nor ardent!
I lived as a young lad; I knew my youth wasted me;
I was neither romantic nor athletic
I lived as an employee; drew a salary but not satisfaction;
I was neither condemned nor rewarded
I lived as a professional, but it was more occasional;

Neither I could deliver nor my profession
I lived as a spouse; it was my life's delightful oasis;
I was neither irresponsible nor adorable
I lived as a lover; always advanced, only to retreat;
I was neither amicable nor endurable
I lived as a thinker; I ignited no sparks in others;
I neither clicked nor did my thinking kick me
I lived as a philosopher; I could joke but not provoke;
I was neither recognized nor banished
I lived as a man; a good-hearted gentleman, unnoticed;
I was neither charming nor harming
I lived as a saint; more due to lack of money and guts;
I could neither preach nor reach

I live now, as a contented person, simple yet complex;
Ever passionate and compassionate

Humour

Boochandi and Pichandi are one of the smartest duo friends made for each other. They do everything together, except a few inevitable things which have to be done alone. Boochandi 50, is a bachelor while Pichandi 40 is unmarried. Although both of them were born on the same day, in the same hospital, in the same city, their parents are different and hence the difference in their present age. Forty years ago, it was rumoured in their school circles that Boochandi's age was extrapolated as 5 when he was one year old. On the other hand, the age of Pichandi was interpolated as one when he was five years old. When this matter was brought to the notice of their parents, they said

"We have one common astrologer by name'Poojyam Sri'. He holds in his hands, a Master's degree in M.A. (Manipulating Art, and he only arrived at these revised ages after steadily studying and searching, so many horoscopes without researching Boochandi and Pichandi's horoscopes for five years".

One day Boochandi and Pichandi visit one of their school days friends 'Machandi'. Machandi is 45 years (but looks like 54 years) and married but is also a bachelor, because he has a Bachelor of Arts degree. His wife (The wife who was married by him) is a woman who had a beautiful name 'SSS 123' kept by her grandparents when she was three hours old. Her parents didn't like this name doubting that SSS stood for Silly, Selfish, and Stupid. So in the next three hundred hours, they secretly amended her name to 'Shri Sthree". Her friends got confused and so started to call her 'Shri 123'.

Shri 123, lost her grandparents when both of them died while trying to live more, due to age-old disease of old age. Her grandmother 'Subbaayee' was 99 years, 9 months, and 9 days when she breathed her last but one breath but was later declared clinically dead by a team of doctors who were qualified Insurance agents. Her grandfather 'Subbaiah' was 111 years, 11 months, and 11 days, died technically when he could not release carbon dioxide in exchange for the oxygen he inhaled. This was confirmed by a team of Surgeons who held diploma certificates in "Operations Management".

Right now Boochandi, Pichandi, and Machandi are locked up in a room, caught in the nostalgia, and are being swept away by the 'excitement amnesia'. The wife of Machandi, 'Shri 123' has started preparing tea for them. Do you know how many cups of tea, she would make?

Three, No. Four, No. Five, No. Six, Yes. Three for BPM objects, one for Shri 123, and two cups for her servant maid, originally named 'Not Two' which was later corrupted and then got corrected as 'Natoo' in her school records.

* * *

Thought
A to Z events during my life until this date

Achieved something
Broken something
Created something
Disliked someone
Earned something
Fought someone
Greeted someone
Helped someone
Inspired someone
Joked something
Kindled someone
Liked something
Missed someone
Noted something
Opted something
Pained someone
Quit something
Rocked sometime
Smiled sometime

Tackled something
Understood someone
Ventured something
Wasted something
Xeroxed something
Yielded something
Zeroed on something

www.ingramcontent.com/pod-product-compliance
Lightning Source LLC
Chambersburg PA
CBHW030023260726
48782CB00025B/294

9798890678041